KID COOPERATION

How to Stop Yelling, Nagging and Pleading and Get Kids to Cooperate

ELIZABETH PANTLEY

Foreword by William Sears, M.D.
Preface by Louise Bates Ames, Ph.D.

NEW HARBINGER PUBLICATIONS, INC.

Publisher's Note

This publication is designed to provide accurate and authoritative information in regard to the subject matter covered. It is sold with the understanding that the publisher is not engaged in rendering psychological, financial, legal, or other professional services. If expert assistance or counseling is needed, the services of a competent professional should be sought.

Distributed in Canada by Raincoast Books

Copyright © 1996 Elizabeth Pantley
New Harbinger Publications, Inc.
5674 Shattuck Avenue
Oakland, CA 94609

Cover design by SHELBY DESIGNS & ILLUSTRATES.
Text design by Tracy Marie Powell.

Library of Congress Catalog Card Number: 95-72223

ISBN-10 1-57224-040-7
ISBN-13 978-1-57224-040-7

FSC
Mixed Sources
Product group from well-managed
forests and other controlled sources

Cert no. SW-COC-002283
www.fsc.org
© 1996 Forest Stewardship Council

New Harbinger Publications' website address: www.newharbinger.com

11   10   09

30   29   28   27   26   25   24

This book is dedicated to my family.

Robert My husband, my love, my true soulmate, the one I know I can always count on to be there for me.

Dolores My mom, my children's beloved "Grama," who blesses our home with her presence and wisdom.

Angela, Vanessa, and David God's gift of love to me, my greatest treasures, and the secret stars of this book.

Michelle My sister, my friend. Thank you for adding your loving touch to this book.

Loren, Sarah, Nicholas, Reneé, Glenn, Amber, and Matthew Thank you for your laughter, love, and support.

Contents

Foreword

How you phrase a request to your child can mean the difference between compliance and defiance. *Kid Cooperation* gives you the tools you need, not only to encourage compliance, but to create a close, loving, and respectful relationship between you and your child.

This is a book about living with children in the day-to-day world. It will help you communicate more effectively with your kids, so that they know you mean what you say, and they clearly understand your expectations. You will learn to present discipline—and consequences for misbehavior—in a context of love and support.

Creating an atmosphere of cooperation is therapeutic for the whole family. Disciplining your child can become a personal discovery in how you yourself were parented. An exasperated mother once told me, "I notice my own mother's voice coming out of my mouth." As you heal the unhealthy parts of yourself, you will find that you're able to be a more loving parent to your child.

Elizabeth teaches parents how to listen to, and control, their anger—how to nip in the bud situations that can push parents over the edge into rage. As you practice the techniques in this book, you'll find that the occasions when you feel really frustrated and angry will grow fewer and farther between.

By taking care of yourself and respecting your own needs, you will be able to take better care of your children. Elizabeth makes a special point of this in Chapter 8. Best of all, after putting Elizabeth's ideas into practice, you'll be much more able to enjoy your children, and to enjoy the experience of being a parent. After all, isn't that the reason why we become parents in the first place?

—William Sears,
Co-author of *The Baby Book*
and *The Discipline Book*

Preface

Direct. Clear. Sensible. Workable. Down-to-earth. Here is a book we have long been waiting for, and one that we heartily welcome. Familiarity with its practical and sage advice could improve almost any family's living situation, making it less stressful and more enjoyable. I guarantee that this book will have a calming effect on any distraught parent.

Books of advice on parenting, scarce indeed early in this century, now abound. Some are splendid, others are less so. *Kid Cooperation* is one of the best. I envy any parent who has the privilege of reading it and learning from it.

The author's advice is appealing to me because it is direct, practical, uncomplicated, consistent, and easy to follow. It does not depend on some complex and possibly questionable theory of human behavior. Rather, it applies directly to you, the parent, and to your own child or children, in your own living situation.

A little boy of our acquaintance once told his mother that the word he hated the very most was "cooperation." Here is a book that tells parents how to make cooperation, even if not always easy, at least possible to achieve.

This book appeals to me, a longtime giver of advice, because so many of the suggestions found here are ones that I know work.

Unlike the pediatrician (back in the days when many pediatricians were trained in medicine, but not in behavior) who advised the mother of a biter to "just bite him back," this author has clearly been around the track a time or two herself. Her advice, whatever the problem, is simple, sound, practical, and workable.

One of her most important and useful points is something that all too many of us sometimes forget. This is that the child's world and point of view and that of his parents are by no means necessarily the same. Children and parents often have very different definitions of the same idea. Thus the parent may say, "Clean your room," and the child interprets the remark as meaning, "Push everything under your bed."

One especially fine section of this book elaborates on the well-known "time out" method of discipline, a method that works because it effectively interrupts the child's negative behavior with space, time, and quiet. Here we find one of the best discussions of time out available.

This book also includes clear, comprehensive, and useful descriptions of many of the more important features of parenting. For instance, "Grandma's Rule," as this author correctly describes it, gives children certain responsibilities and privileges as members of the family. But it emphasizes that they must earn the privileges by first fulfilling certain responsibilities. All too many children today want the privileges free and clear.

A fine and very specific chapter on "Keys to Successful Parenting," like so much of the advice to be found here, could actually bring about a measurable change and improvement in any parent's handling of his or her child. The entire book is full of nuggets, plain and simple, but worth their weight in the proverbial gold.

One of the great beauties of this fine book is that it makes the difficult sound easy, or at least plausible. It does not fudge or dodge or gloss over. It admits that family living is not always smooth or easy. But it gives a parent the feeling that even the most difficult child-rearing problems are quite common and can be coped with. It presents the often difficult problems of daily living with our young as intriguing challenges, rather than hopeless tasks. Kid Cooperation *teaches you how to be the parent your child deserves.*

—Louise Bates Ames, Ph.D.
Associate Director, Gesell Institute of Human
Development

Acknowledgments

I would like to express my gratitude to the following people for their heartfelt support and encouragement. Their love and professionalism has added meaning to this book, my classes, and my life.

Rona L. Levy, M.S.W., Ph.D., M.P.H.

Dr. Levy received her graduate degrees in psychology, social work, and public health from the University of Michigan. She has been a professor at the University of Washington in Seattle since 1975, and has extensive publications in both clinical and research issues. Dr. Levy also has a part-time clinical practice where she works with individuals and families experiencing a wide range of problems, including issues related to children. She lives in Washington with her husband, Andrew D. Feld, M.D., and their three children, Shara, Kayla, and Lauren.

M. Alexander MacDonald

Mr. MacDonald is the President of The LYFE Enhancement Company, a Seattle-based human resource consulting firm. He is an internationally known speaker in the field of personal motivation. His background includes a degree in psychology, and graduate work in International Relations at Oxford University.

Kristen Knox, M.D., M.P.H.

Dr. Knox is a family doctor who received both of her advanced degrees, in medicine and public health, from UCLA. She has many years' experience caring for children and families in the United States and developing countries. She practices in Kirkland, Washington where she lives with her husband, Kevin Makela and their son, Anders.

Christine Jester

Ms. Jester received her training in art and elementary education from Eastern Illinois University, and her Montessori Certification from University of Puget Sound. She is co-director at Countryside Montessori School, which she opened in 1983. She is the mother of three children, and has one grandchild.

My heartfelt thanks to Barbara Quick for her editing expertise, and to Patrick Fanning, Matt McKay, Kirk Johnson, Kristin Beck, Lauren Docket, and everyone at New Harbinger Publications for making this book possible.

Introduction

Why Did I Write This Book?

When I was about to become a parent for the first time, I realized just how little I knew about children. All the knowledge, skill, and wisdom I had accumulated in the first 29 years of my life would not serve me well when it came to raising a child. When I actually brought my first baby home from the hospital, I was reduced to a nervous, worried, incompetent ninny. I had no idea how to care for a newborn. Sure, I had read books about the subject, but this was a real baby here. To make matters worse, she choked and stopped breathing for the longest seven seconds of my life on her first night home from the hospital—which added fear to my growing repertoire of emotions. As a matter of fact, I didn't bathe her until six days later, because I felt so incapable of handling my little five-pound package. Many years and two more children later, I now feel confident, competent, and capable . . . most of the time. Parenting is still a challenge, because every year brings new ages and stages, new problems, and new issues to deal with.

Somewhere along my early parenting experience, I began a support group of parents, which focused on raising children from birth to age six—specifically, on how we could encourage our children's development during these early years. This support group turned into a full-time business I called "Better Beginnings," aimed at providing parents with the knowledge and tools to nurture their young children's development.

Parents everywhere—with children from toddlers to teenagers—are looking for answers to the same question: "How can I raise my child effectively, day-by-day, without yelling, nagging, and pleading?"

I have found great answers to this question, in bits and pieces, through a wide range of classes, books, tapes, and experiences. I have made suggestions to parents, and gathered data on what works, and what doesn't. During the discussion portion of each class, I change from teacher to student. I listen carefully to the many stories that parents tell, and I have thought deeply about the subtle nuances that make all families different, yet the same. I have had the opportunity to see families come closer together. I have seen many parents learn skills that made them more confident and effective with their children. It has been an exciting journey.

Recently five of my clients called to tell me about a talk-show special on discipline. As I watched the show, my heart ached to see parents who loved their children deeply, but talked of "losing it" on a regular basis because they just didn't know what to do when misbehavior occurred. I heard one young couple beg for help because they were spanking their two little girls on a daily basis, yet still not achieving cooperation from them. I watched families full of confusion and self-doubt. My mother was watching with me, and she had to leave the room when a home video was shown of parents using a wooden "rod" to spank their two-year-old daughter when she refused to pick up her blocks. I wanted to shout at these parents, *there is a better way!*

The more I studied parenting, the harder it was for me to watch parents engaged in an unnecessary struggle with their children. There are so many wonderful books and articles written about discipline. There are many wonderful parenting programs, classes, and tapes available through bookstores, libraries, and schools. There are so many great ideas out there. That's when it hit me: since parenting is my business, I can take hours every day to study, read, and learn. But that's not so for most parents. Life is busy, too busy to research volumes to get the answers to your current child-rearing problems. That was the moment when I became passionate about writing a book, a book that would bring together the best of the best ideas I had accumulated through thousands of different sources and experiences. So here it is. My sincere hope is that you'll find many practical, effective ideas in this book that will help you be a calmer, more peaceful, and loving parent—a parent who's in control and confident and working toward the goal of raising happy, confident, self-disciplined children.

Parenting: A Tough Job

Many years ago, before I had children, I had a friend named Susan. She was a CPA and a former teacher. She ran marathons. She raised horses. She was very intelligent and capable. Susan handled our accounting, so I saw her every few months. She had just returned from a six-month maternity leave to have her first baby. After we said hello, Susan collapsed into a chair, looked up at me, and said, "I've done many things in my life. I've traveled in the Far East. I've ridden horses that were supposed to be unridable. I supported myself through college, and built a successful career from scratch. I married the guy who swore up and down that he never wanted to get married. Let me tell you something. Being a mom is the toughest job I've ever had." "She's got to be joking!" I thought. "Her baby's only six months old. How hard could that be?"

How hard? As they say, ignorance is bliss. I have since had three children of my own. And, as you already know, *have I learned!* Yes, Susan, wherever you are today, you were right. Being a parent is the toughest job on earth.

Parenting. Raising children. Raising *human beings*. It is the most important job you'll ever have. Parenting is not only challenging, but scary. It can be fulfilling, exciting, and often frustrating. Parenting is tougher than most jobs, because we have so little training, yet the results are so much more important. If you're in sales and you lose a sale, your check is smaller. If you're in accounting and the books don't balance, you stay late to find your error and correct it. If you're a chef and the cake goes flat, you make another. In parenting, if you fail, your child—that person you love most in the world—could suffer for the rest of his or her life. Your relationship with your child will suffer, and so will your marriage. You may lose friends if your children are impossible to be around. You may become increasingly isolated, and your self-esteem may go down the drain. Your parenting style affects just about every other aspect of your life—even your relationship to your work.

There can be real, life-long satisfaction and meaning in raising a child and doing the very best job you can. By being a more knowledgeable, in-control parent, you can maximize that meaning and satisfaction; and you will also give your children a gift that will confer blessings on them for the rest of their lives.

Why Didn't Grandma Take Parenting Classes?

Why is it that our parents and our grandparents never took parenting classes? Why is it that they never read parenting books? They never sat around and discussed parenting, because the term *parenting* never even existed back then. Raising kids was just something everyone did. People grew up in large families, and lived close to relatives: dealing with small children was a normal, everyday occurrence. I was recently speaking to a man in his late sixties, a grandparent of seven. When I answered his question of, "What do you do for a living?" with "I teach parenting classes," he just about choked on his bread. "Humph," he said when he'd recovered. "Kids. You just raise 'em." However, by the time we ended our discussion about the difference between parenting today and 50 years ago, the man admitted that you couldn't pay him to raise his seven grandchildren in today's world.

Our lives have changed. Society has changed. In the "olden days" (as my daughter calls them), society was better equipped to uphold and support the family. Lines of authority were clear. Children respected and listened to their parents and teachers. Everyone except "the criminal element" respected police officers and other people in positions of authority. Families lived closer together. Divorce was rare. Most moms stayed at home, and most dads were the breadwinners. Television filled our homes with "Ozzie and Harriet," "Leave It to Beaver," "Captain Kangaroo," and "Donna Reed" baking pies in her starched white apron over her tidy dress and high-heeled shoes. Even though we know increasingly the extent to which these picture-perfect television families were myths much more than reflections of reality in America at the time; and even though we also know that some moms of this era were alcoholics, and some dads were child abusers—still the typical problems of the era never even approached the severity of the problems and challenges our kids face now. Disciplinary problems of the fifties and sixties in our schools were likely to involve such minor infractions as late homework, gum-chewing, talking in class, or cutting in line. Very few middle-class kids tried drugs, and drinking a can of beer was considered daring. The occasional teenager who got pregnant was hustled off to live with Aunt Martha for a year, and nobody was ever told why. Kids had to worry about pregnancy, not death, resulting from promiscuity. In video- and computer-free homes, most kids chose to spend their free time playing outside—tag, cowboys and Indians, kick the can, and climbing trees.

Where are we today? Our entire notion of what constitutes a family has changed. Only half of all children in the U.S. today will live with both parents until graduation. In most families, both Mom and Dad work outside the home, and have many obligations taking up time and energy that used to be dedicated exclusively to child-rearing. Children test the authority of their parents and teachers more than at any time in our history.

Television fills our homes with the cynicism of shows like "The Simpsons," and the insanity of shows like "Beavis and Butthead." Children who watch network TV—and most do—are mesmerized by programs filled with violence, sex, and negative role models. The problems of schoolchildren today are likely to involve drugs and life-threatening violence. Teen pregnancy and suicide, far from being the rare occurrences they once were, are now common and even epidemic in some schools. According to the U.S. Census Bureau's report of 1992, by the time our youth are 25 years old, 48 percent of them try drugs, and 86 percent try alcohol. Even among 12- to 17-year-old American children, drugs are used by over 10 percent and alcohol by almost 40 percent. Overall scholastic achievement scores in public schools across the country have dropped. Kids spend much of the time they used to spend out of doors playing Nintendo and watching TV.

Is there any doubt in your mind that it's harder to parent a child today?

The Good News

The good news is that even in today's world you can establish parental authority in your home, and nurture well-behaved kids with good manners and healthy self-esteem. You can even enjoy the process of parenting your children on a day-to-day basis. It will take a commitment on your part. It will take practice and patience. It will take time. The hundreds of parents whom I've taught through my parenting classes report that having the requisite knowledge and skills makes parenting a rewarding, fulfilling, and sometimes even a peaceful job.

This book is filled with practical, purposeful parenting ideas. Real ideas for real families. Skills that you can use in your daily interactions with your children. Practical ideas for getting kids to cooperate, ending sibling fights, boosting children's self-esteem, and handling discipline issues with knowledge and authority.

Parenting *is* the toughest job you'll ever have. But if you are prepared—if you have the tools and the skills to parent—it can be the most fulfilling, exciting job you'll ever have, with the end result being children who grow into happy, fulfilled, self-motivated, and secure adults. Isn't that every parent's dream?

How to Make the Most of This Book

A lot of parenting books present a general philosophy and theories without giving a clue about how to customize the information so that you can use it to make positive changes in your family. In the hustle of daily living, many parents just don't have the time to do the analysis and examination this involves. In *Kid Cooperation*, I've been able to offer you specific skills that are easy to learn, easy to use, and—most importantly—ready for you to use *today*.

Chapters 2–8 have "reminder pages" at the end, summing up the skills contained in each chapter. Photocopy these pages, and post them somewhere conspicuous as you work your way through the skills presented. You might want to post just one reminder page for several weeks before adding another—let the skills sink in slowly, and give yourself and your family sufficient time to adjust. Once you make these techniques your own, you'll have them at your fingertips for the rest of your life (you'll even be able to use them with your grandchildren).

1

What's Your Parenting Style?

The quiz on page 8 will identify your parenting style, providing you with a starting point from which to work. In order to become a better parent, you need to understand *how you parent now*. It can be hard to see yourself objectively. This quiz will help.

Read each question, and choose the answer that seems *most like what you think you would do* in that case. Even if your child is older or younger than the child in the example, you can still answer based on what you *think you would do.*

Don't give the answer you *think* is right. Instead, put yourself in the situation and give the answer that best reflects what you would actually do. You don't have to show your answers to anyone. This quiz was created to help you take an honest look at how you parent, so that you can pinpoint the areas in which you need to create change.

Jot down your answers on a piece of paper. After the quiz, I'll show you how to score your answers. The quiz will help you identify your current parenting style, and specify ways to adjust your style in more positive directions, if need be. If you have a partner, it would be useful for both of you to take the quiz separately, and compare your answers when you're through. Just photocopy the pages containing the quiz.

Quiz: What's Your Parenting Style?

1. **Your child is throwing a *major tantrum* in the grocery store because she wants the free cookie being offered from the bakery. You said no, because it's just before dinner. Everyone is staring at you and the bakery clerk is smiling and holding out the cookie. You**

    A   Let her have the cookie.

    B   Take her by the hand and quickly walk away from the bakery while explaining, "Honey, I know you would like a cookie. I know it's hard to say no when someone is offering you a treat. But it's almost dinnertime, and a cookie will spoil your appetite. You can have a cookie at home after dinner. Please stop crying."

    C   Take her by the hand, or pick her up, and go to a quiet corner or out to the car, where you sit until she is calm and ready to re-enter the store.

    D   Yell at her, "I will not have this! Bad girl!" Give her a smack on the bottom and say, "Stop this behavior right now, young lady!"

2. **You are in the kitchen preparing dinner. Your children are in the family room fighting over a toy. Suddenly, you hear a scream and a cry. One child yells, "He took my toy!" The other yells, "He started it!" You**

    A   Mumble to yourself, "Why can't these kids ever get along?"

    B   Listen to the details, then discipline the wrongdoer.

    C   Suggest they work it out together.

    D   Send one (or both) to their rooms for a "time out."

3. **Your child wants to go outside and play. You say no, because it's almost time for dinner. Your child says, "Oh, please!" You say no again. Your child says, "I *promise* I'll only play for 10 minutes and I'll come right in. I even have my watch on. I'll stay in the yard. Please?" You**

    A   Say, "Okay. But make sure you're back in 10 minutes."

    B   Explain to your child that it's almost dinnertime, and that whenever you allow outside play before dinner, everyone always comes to the table late, and dinner gets cold. Explain that you are not trying to be mean, you just want everyone to sit down to dinner together. Your child points out that there are still 15 minutes before dinner, and he'll play right in the backyard. You figure that's reasonable, so you say, "Okay, just come when I call."

C Say, "You may play outside *after* dinner." When your child continues to plead, you say (again), "You may play outside *after* dinner."

D Say, "Stop nagging me." When your child continues to whine, you say, "That's it. Go to your room. I've had it with your whining and fussing—no TV for you tonight."

4. **Your child dawdles and loses track of the time and misses the school bus. You**

    A Drive your child to school.

    B Drive your child to school. During the trip, you explain the importance of being organized and following a routine in the morning. Extract a promise for better cooperation tomorrow.

    C This wouldn't happen. You have a very specific morning routine that everyone adheres to.

    D Say, "That's what you get for dawdling. Now you'll have to walk to school. Get your coat."

5. **Your toddler is constantly touching the control knobs on the stereo. You have repeatedly said no. You are getting tired of the battle. You**

    A Ignore him. He's not going to hurt the stereo anyway.

    B Buy him a toy stereo to play with.

    C Move the stereo to a higher shelf.

    D Smack his hand every time he touches the knobs. He will learn to leave it alone.

6. **Your child is six years old. As usual, you walk into the family room to see toys and books littering every square inch. You have had enough of this mess. You**

    A Take a deep breath and start cleaning the room.

    B Sit down with your child at the table. Explain that you cannot live with the mess anymore. Ask your child for suggestions to solve the ongoing problem.

    C Say to your child, "Toys belong in the toy-box and books belong on the shelf. I expect this room to be straightened out before dinner."

D   Grab a garbage bag and start filling it while yelling at your child, "I've had enough! This stuff is going to the trash!"

7. **It's 11:30 PM. Your ten-year-old is sleeping. You notice that the dog still has not been fed dinner or taken outside. This is a daily problem. You**

A   Feed and walk the dog while muttering angrily about your child's lack of responsibility.

B   Feed the dog and let him outside. In the morning, you talk to your child about the responsibilities of pet ownership.

C   Feed the dog and let him outside. The next day, you help your child create a daily chart to use as a reminder. You include a consequence for failure to do the job. You discuss the chart with your child, and put the plan into action.

D   Wake your child up and say, "Get downstairs and feed and walk your dog! I'm sick and tired of having to do it for you."

8. **Your eight-year-old's goldfish dies because it has not been fed. Feeding the fish is your child's responsibility. Your child is lying on the sofa sobbing. You**

A   Say, "Please don't cry honey. I'll buy you another goldfish. I'll even buy you two new goldfish!"

B   Feel guilty because you didn't feed the fish for your child.

C   Sit beside your child and say, "It sure can be sad to lose a pet." You show sadness for your child, but this is one of those lessons of life that just have to be learned.

D   Say, "Maybe this will teach you to take some responsibility for your chores in future. If you'd fed your fish, it wouldn't have died."

9. **For the second time this month, your ten-year-old son loses his school notebook. You**

A   Buy him another one, and ask him to be more careful.

B   Talk to him about responsibility. Explain the cost of a new notebook. Teach him how to take better care of his property. Make him promise to be more careful.

C   Let him use loose-leaf paper for now, and save up his allowance to buy a new notebook.

D   Take away a privilege—like watching TV, or playing outside.

10. **Several of your 17-year-old son's friends have pierced their nostrils, and now proudly display nose-rings. Your son wants to pierce his nose, too. You**

   A   Say no, but he does it anyway.

   B   Say no. But he asks you every day. He promises he'll never wear it to family gatherings. He promises he won't wear it to school. He promises it will just be a little-tiny-itty-bitty one. You say okay.

   C   Tell him you sure don't like the idea, and explain why, but tell him that he needs to make his own decision.

   D   Absolutely forbid it! No son of yours is going to wear a nose-ring!

11. **It's Saturday and it's raining outside. Your six-year-old wants to go out in the yard and play in the puddles. You**

   A   Say no. Then she tells you that the neighbor kids are outside. And she'll be careful. She says it's really warm out, and it's only drizzling, anyway. You say okay.

   B   Tell her that it's raining, and she'll have to wait until it stops. Then you find something else to occupy her.

   C   Say, "Sure. Please get a towel and some dry clothes, and put them by the door for when you come in."

   D   Say, "You silly kid. It's raining out. Go find something to do inside."

12. **You walk into the room and catch your three-year-old writing on the wall with her crayons. You**

   A   Say, "Oh, dear! Look what you've done! Now I have to clean up this mess. What's the landlord going to say? You're not supposed to write on the walls! Go play in the living room while I clean this up!"

   B   Say, "What a mess! It's my fault for leaving you in here with the crayons and no paper. Please don't do this again."

   C   Say firmly, "We do *not* write on walls. We write on *paper*. Now, let's get a sponge, and you can help me wash the crayon off the wall."

   D   Slap her hand while yelling, "No! Bad girl!" and send her to her room.

Scoring Your Answers

Give yourself:

> 0 points for each A
>
> 2 points for each B
>
> 4 points for each C
>
> 6 points for each D

Calculate your total. Read the description below that matches your score level. If you score close to another category, review that one, too. (You may find it helpful to read all the categories, since many of us slip into a different parenting style once in a while.)

0–14 Points: The Permissive Parent

You probably find it difficult to say no to your child. Perhaps you are too easily swayed by your persistent child. You may be frustrated and angry because you feel you have so little control over your child. As difficult as this may make your life, rest assured that you are *not* a bad parent or a weak person. You just need to acquire some new skills. Once you have learned strategies for enlisting your child's cooperation, and handling misbehavior, you will enjoy parenting—and your child—much, much more. Hang in there! Commit some time to reading this book and practicing the skills described. In a few short months, you will be able to take control of your family life and boost your own self-esteem.

14–36 Points: The Democratic Parent

You've been trying, and most likely have had some success, in enlisting your child's cooperation. You treat your child as an equal human being and you try to be fair and consistent. So why do you still feel as if you could do a better job? Why is it that your child still misbehaves so frequently? Most likely, your style of parenting is holding you back. You are trying *too hard* to be perfect in every situation, and to always be fair and reasonable. You are trying too hard to treat your child as an equal. You think too hard about the long-term results when you discipline your child—Am I being too harsh? Am I being too easy? Is this the right thing to do? You would do well to *talk less* and *act more*. It would benefit you to understand that as parent and child, you are *not* equals. You must be the authority in your home during these growing years, and as such, set up the foundation for the friendship that will form between you and your child when your child is an adult.

A very common trait of the democratic parent is the tendency to lecture, teach, and moralize to the point of forcing your child to tune you out (a phenomenon called "parent-deafness").

Take heart! Commit some time to reading this book and practicing the skills presented here. In a few short months, you will feel more in control, more like a leader, and your children's respect for you will increase tenfold.

36–50 Points: The Balanced Parent

Why are *you* reading this book? Seriously—you are doing a great job (or else you fibbed on the quiz!). You must have read some parenting books, or taken a parenting class. Good for you!

As a balanced parent, you may have a problem with being too hard on yourself. Your abundance of knowledge regarding child-rearing may set you up to feel like a failure when you have a bad moment or a bad day. Keep in mind that there is no such thing as a perfect parent; and that your overall parenting style is both healthy and productive.

There is no job more important than raising your child. The more knowledge you have, the more your child will benefit. I think you will find some wonderful ideas here, and perhaps a few important new skills that will refine your parenting style. I know that for me, the more I know and the more I learn, the more confident and capable I feel. Keep up the good work!

50–72 Points: The Autocratic Parent

Yes, Sir, Captain, Sir! I would guess that one of the two following situations describes your home:

If your child is younger than 15, you've got a pretty good kid. Your child behaves—because he knows he must. There is a hidden negative here, though. A child who behaves out of fear of punishment, or desire for a reward, does not develop the inner discipline that will serve him when his parent is not breathing down his neck. Children with autocratic parents can learn to resent authority, and often have an inability to express what's on their minds. They may also become dependent on having someone else tell them what to do—a dangerous trait that leads children to follow the wrong crowd, or join a gang. In addition, an autocratic stance toward your child can erode your parent-child bond and block effective communication.

If your child is older than 15, you're probably facing new problems. An autocratic style tends to create rebellion in an adolescent, and the methods that have kept him in line up to now no longer work.

If neither of the previous descriptions describes you, does this: you aren't having much fun parenting. You find yourself yelling too much, hitting too much, and feeling too much stress. You *try* to make your kids mind, but your efforts only succeed in making you angry.

Hang in there! You have some right ideas that need some refinement and control. Once you have read this book, and practiced the skills presented, you will find both your blood pressure and the volume of your voice going down. You will enjoy your kids more, and they will enjoy you more.

Now What?

You now have a picture of your own parenting style—something you may not have thought much about until now. Knowing your style is an effective starting point for positive growth. Once you have evaluated your strengths and weaknesses, you can make the changes required to help you be a more balanced parent.

If you and your partner have each taken the quiz, you may wish to review your scores together, and discuss the differences and similarities in your styles. It is helpful for partners to find a certain level of agreement on issues involving discipline and expectations. Reading this book together will open the door for discussion that can lead to greater consensus and teamwork in raising your children.

When using the guidelines in this book to improve your parenting style, remember to allow yourself time and practice in making changes. You have a lifetime of experiences, memories, and impressions that have formed your current parenting style. It will take patience, practice, and persistence to change. You will know that your time and effort have been well worth it when you see the positive impact these changes have on your family.

2

The Keys to
Successful Parenting

The Balanced Family

Now that you have been able to identify your parenting style, you can begin to really think about how you are parenting now, and what changes you would like to make toward a more balanced style. The goal is to identify your weak points, and learn new skills that will enable you to take control of your family life, and find more enjoyment in parenting your children.

The Balanced Family structure is based on four basic rules:

- Parents—Take Charge!

- Parents—Think!

- When You Say It, Mean It!

- Use Skill!

Rule 1: Parents—Take Charge!

King Edward VII, after a trip to America, said, "The thing that impresses me most about America is the way parents obey their children." So often, parents are unknowingly and unconsciously controlled by their children. Parents may wish and hope that their children will behave, but somehow lack the skills and knowledge to follow through on their hopes. Most often, these parents are not even aware of what is happening to them, even when they can point out when it's happening to *other* parents. These are some examples from a recent trip to the park:

It is a sunny summer day. I decide to take my three children and my sister's two children to the park. As I sit on a park bench and read my book (on parenting, what else?), I occasionally look up to view the parenting styles of other people in the park. I see a mother and daughter (around age nine). The daughter is on the top of the slide and calls out:

Daughter: Ma! I want some of that juice.

Mother: Okay, honey. (Brings the juice over to the slide, and hands it to her daughter along with a granola bar)

Daughter: I just asked for *juice*. (Tosses the granola bar back at her mother)

Mother: (Not even noticing the disrespect) I don't think it's safe for you to be up there with your rollerblades on.

Daughter: I'm fine, Mom.

Mother: I sure wish you'd come down.

Daughter: I'm being careful.

Mother: Oh, okay.

I shake my head and return to my book. A few minutes later, I see two dads with their three-year-old girls. One of the girls takes her shoes off. The other sits down to do the same.

Father: You know our rule: shoes stay on at the park.

Daughter: But Susie has her shoes off!

Father: I know. But that's our rule.

Daughter: (Starts to cry) But I want mine off, too!

Father: But you *know* the rule!

Daughter: (Crying) Pleeeeease, Daddy!

Father: (Shrugging his shoulders) Oh, I guess it would be all right.

I could just cry! It's sad when a parent starts off so right, but then allows a fussing, whining child to win the battle! And speaking of battles, I turn my head to watch what's happening at the swings.

A mother is pushing her two sons (ages three and six) on the swings.

Mother:	Wow. It's getting late. We'd better go.
Son 1:	Not now! I want to stay!
Son 2:	Me too!
Mother:	But I have to go home and make dinner.
Son 1:	Not yet, Mom.
Mother:	Well, five more minutes. (Continues to push the swings)
Mother:	Okay, boys, time to go.
Son 2:	Ten more pushes!
Mother:	Five more.
Sons 1 & 2:	Ten more—p l e a s e !
Mother:	One-two-three-four-five-six-seven-eight-nine-ten. Let's go.
Son 1:	One more minute.
Mother:	Now. (Boys keep swinging)
Mother:	(Yelling) I said *now*. Get off those swings. Time to go! Why don't you boys ever listen to me?

Did you see, maybe, a little bit of yourself in these parents? (A lot? Hey! Was that *you* at the park?) In the parenting classes I teach, we use role-play from scripts to demonstrate the *lack of* versus the *use of* different skills. We always call people like these in the park "Parent 1." (The parent *with* skill is called "Parent 2.") At a Montessori school where I taught, the owner (who is also the mother of three grown children) arrived at the second class, and wrote her name on her name tag as *Julie, Parent 1!*

Okay, so we're not perfect, nor will we ever be. But how, oh how, can we be a parent in control of the daily situations that occur with our children?

Step 1: Attitude Check

Say this with me, out loud, three times: **I am the parent. I am in charge.**

Do you believe it? Or do you still feel like your parents' child? Do you still question your decisions? Do you worry a lot about your mistakes? The first step toward improving your situation is to change your attitude. Of course, you *will* make mistakes, everyone does. But if you are the kind of parent who reads a book like this, then your efforts, your skills, and your love for your child will far outweigh any mistakes you make. An overall solid parenting style will more than compensate for a few mistakes. The problem comes when you repeat a mistake over and over. A very common mistake is allowing a child to be in control.

> Dr. Wilson received a call from Kara Smith. Her eight-month-old baby was sick, and she wanted to know if she should bring him in to the office. Dr. Wilson asked what the baby's temperature was. Kara replied, "I don't know. He won't let me take it."

> Chris Young was complaining to her husband, "Kenneth makes me so angry! He knows his curfew is 10:00, but every night he comes in late. He always has an excuse. It's always as if he comes home late just to show me that he can do what he wants."

In these examples, the parent is allowing the child to have control of a situation in which the control should belong to the parent. This happens to loving parents who neglect to make a conscious decision to be the leader in the relationship with their child.

Decide here and now that you will be in charge. It is not only your right, it is your responsibility. Your children *need* you to parent them effectively. They are counting on you to guide them into adulthood.

Expect Your Children to Obey You

Your expectation alone will carry weight in the eyes of your children. When you expect your children to obey, you will act differently. You will have an inner strength that your children will rely on. *Expecting* your children to obey is much different than *wishing* that your children would obey. Remember the mom with the nine-year-old on the slide with rollerblades? The mom said, *"I don't think it's safe for you to be up there. I sure wish you'd come down."* That's a very typical parental request. Couple it with that hopeful add-on, "Okay?" and you have yourself an ineffective request. Other "wishing" statements start out: "Would you like to . . . ?" or "It would be nice if you . . . " or "Don't you think you should?" When you expect your children to obey, your vocabulary changes. For example, try these alternatives when asking a child to do something. (Oops—should I have said *telling* instead of *asking?* I think my subconscious still finds it hard to let me feel like the parent in control!)

Make a Statement

"It's not safe up there with your rollerblades on. Come down, or take them off."

"Boys, we are leaving the park in 5 minutes."

Please X

"Please take out the garbage."
"Please put away your books."

When You X, You May X

"When you have finished your homework, you may go out and play."
"When you have cleared the table, you may have dessert."

In the chapter on cooperation, I'll present more ways of using powerful language to show your child, in a loving, respectful way, that you are in control.

Step 2: No Guilt, No Excuses, No Explanations

We undermine many of our decisions by allowing guilt to creep in. The dad with the three-year-old in the park who let his daughter take off her shoes despite their "shoes-on-in-the-park" rule gave in because his little girl cried, and her friend had her shoes off. So Dad felt guilty and worried about his daughter's immediate happiness. Is making our children happy our most important job? I don't think so. Consider this:

Our Most Important Job Is Not to Make Our Children Happy, But to Prepare Them for Life

Life is not always fair. Life is not always consistent. Many of our family rules are created because they reflect what we as a family believe in, not what society as a whole believes in. As an example, not all six-year-olds go to bed at the same time. Some go to bed at 8:00. Some at 9:00. Some at 10:00. Some kids are allowed to run around barefoot, some are not. Some kids must make their beds, some don't have to. Some kids walk to school, some ride the bus. Which rules are the right rules? Which are the best rules? They *all* are. Families are different. Families' needs are different. Families' goals are different. It's okay for families' rules to be different, too.

Once you decide what *your* family's rules are, you need to feel comfortable enforcing them. Don't worry about what the neighbors are doing. Don't worry if your rules aren't perfect. Don't overthink your decisions: as a matter of fact, if you look hard enough, you can find an expert somewhere who will agree that whatever you have decided is right.

Because I Said So!

Didn't you just *hate* it when your parents said that? I did, too. Even so, believe it or not, I occasionally use this line on my kids, because, sometimes, it's the only real reason!

Child:	Why do I have to come in now?
Parent:	Because I said so.
Child:	Why can't I have this?
Parent:	Because I said so.
Child:	Why do I have to go to bed at 8:30?
Parent:	Because I said so.

There's another good reason to use this old standby. When kids ask "Why?" usually they don't *really* want a reason, they want you to change your mind. Typically, the more reasons you give, the harder they fight:

Mom:	Time to go now.
Child:	Why?
Mom:	Because it's getting late. We need to go home.
Child:	Why?
Mom:	Because I have to make dinner.
Child:	I'm not hungry.
Mom:	I am.
Child:	Can't you have a granola bar?
Mom:	I don't want a granola bar, I want dinner.
Child:	Well, how about five more minutes? (and on and on and on and on . . .)

Consider instead:

Mom:	Time to go now.
Child:	Why?
Mom:	Because I said so.

Yes, children need explanations for rules and limits to give them the sense that you're not completely arbitrary. However, they don't need a reason for *everything*. When is it okay not to explain? One: Your child already knows the reason, and is just asking as a way to stall. Two: The reason is too complex for your child to understand. Three: Giving the reason will just cause an endless argument.

If "Because I said so" sticks in your throat, try one of these alternatives:

Child:	Why?
Parent:	Because I am the parent and it's my job to make this decision.

Child:	Why?
Parent:	Because I am the adult and I have more experience than you do.
Child:	Why?
Parent:	For many reasons that we are not going to discuss right now.

Whatever you say, it's important to acknowledge the fact that as a parent you are ultimately in control. This does not mean, of course, that you will control everything your children do. A very important part of maintaining your control is to understand that your goal is to prepare your children for life—on their own. This means that as your children grow, you need to give them certain freedoms, along with the responsibilities that go with those freedoms.

When a young tree is first planted, it is held up by two sticks and pieces of rope. As the young tree becomes stronger, and is able to stand alone, the sticks must be removed to allow the tree freedom and room to grow strong. A child, like a young tree, must have the support of his parents while young, like the sticks of support for the tree. As time goes on, he must learn to stand alone, but the memory and direction of the sticks of support will determine how well the child, like the tree, grows to his full potential.

Rule 2: Parents—Think!

Often, when in the role of parent, the tendency is to go with the flow. That is, parents often make decisions and invent rules on the run. They may never really think in advance about their parenting style, specific skills, or household rules. When they see their children doing something they don't like or that's dangerous, they swoop down and say, "Stop!" When their children make an unreasonable request, they say "No!" When a repeated misbehavior occurs, they tend to babble, flap, and whine.

The problem with going with the flow is that you often end up in the rapids, and sometimes even go over the waterfall. Someone once said, "If you fail to plan, you plan to fail." This is so very true when raising a child. If you don't think, if you don't plan, then you can get caught up in the emotions of the moment, and your decisions are going to be less than ideal.

The good news is that *thousands* of parents and professionals have paved the way for you. Take advantage of their experience! Reading books and articles and taking classes will give you the skills and knowledge you need to create a parenting plan that really works. That way, when you see your children doing something you don't like, you can reach into your bag of skills and find an appropriate way to stop the behavior and teach a lesson.

When your children make an unreasonable request, you can be prepared to answer, and not be caught off-guard. When a repeated misbehavior occurs, you can think back to the many examples and ideas you have heard, and come up with a workable solution.

Rule 3: When You Say It, Mean It!

Do you want to do a fascinating experiment? All you need is a tape recorder and a blank tape. Put the recorder in the kitchen, and when you are sharing a meal with your children, turn it on. (Even better, let your spouse or a friend turn it on when you are unaware.) Then sit back and really listen to what happens. You will probably be surprised. A typical parent's comments during an hour-long meal might go something like this:

"Kevin, stop poking your brother. . . ."

"I said, stop poking your brother! . . ."

"Kevin! Do you need to go to time out? Stop poking your brother! . . ."

"What is wrong with you today! Stop that poking! . . ."

"Will you stop that! . . ."

With all the empty words this parent was using, it would have been better not to have even *mentioned* the poking in the first place. How would this exchange be transformed if the parent really meant what was said?

"Kevin, stop poking your brother. . ."

"I asked you to stop poking your brother. Now move your seat over here!"

Children know exactly what number of requests their parents will make before they *really* mean it. They know through experience at just what point they should do what you tell them to do. Consider this example:

Parent:	Aaron, time to come in for dinner.
Child:	(To friend) It's almost my dinnertime.
Parent:	(Five minutes later) Aaron, come in and wash up for dinner!
Friend:	Do you have to go in now?
Child:	No. Not yet.
Parent:	(Five minutes later) Aaron! Dinner is getting cold! Get in here.
Child:	(To friend) I'm gonna have to go in soon.

Parent:	(Three minutes later, *yelling*) Aaron Matthew, get in this house!
Child:	(To friend) Dinnertime! See ya later . . .

Are you a "Ten" parent? Does your child wait until you have asked ten times, your voice is high, your face is red, and your veins are sticking out on your neck before he listens? Could this be because your actions haven't matched your words? Does "Come in now!" really mean "This is a ten-minute warning"? Does "Turn off the TV!" mean "You have to turn off the TV after the next commercial"? Does "Get ready for bed!" mean "You should start *thinking* about getting ready for bed"?

I often hear parents ask their children three or four times to do something. Then, when the child has not cooperated, they yell, "Do it now! And I mean it!" I always wonder why they just didn't mean it the first time. Here's a plan for meaning what you say:

Step 1: Think

Think before you talk. Say only what you are willing to follow up on.

Step 2: Warn

Give one warning.

Step 3: Act

Follow through to physically help your child carry out the desired action.

This example will clarify how the plan works:

Parent:	(Thinking: We have to leave now. I'll let James play for five more minutes.) James. We are leaving in five minutes.
Parent:	(Five minutes later) Please put your shoes on—time to go.
Parent:	(One minute later) James, shoes!
Parent:	(One minute later; picks up shoes in one hand, takes James' hand, and walks him to the car in stocking feet)

When you first change from being a "Ten" parent to a "One" parent, you can expect some real resistance on the part of your child. You will be tested. At first, your child won't believe that you have changed. This is a critical juncture: if you don't follow through *every time*, your child will see that nothing has really changed. If you do follow through every time, your child will catch on that "things are really different around here now!" Soon enough, when you talk you *will* be heard.

Rule 4: Use Skill!

It becomes so much easier to parent when you rely upon skill rather than going with the flow. A parent who has skill has a plan. A parent who has skill has options. A parent who has skill can be calmer and more peaceful. Having skill is the real key to becoming a balanced parent.

When I first started to take parenting classes and learn skills, I felt very awkward with them. I kept reminder cards taped to the front of my refrigerator. In times of crisis, I actually ran over to the refrigerator and read my reminder cards before making a decision about what to do. Over time, I read my reminder cards less and less, and the skills became more and more natural. Eventually, the skills became a part of me, and I was able to remember the key rules as I went about the daily task of raising my children. Now I have lots of options whenever I need to gain my children's cooperation, control an undesired behavior, or deal with an everyday parenting problem.

This book will present you with many skills—or keys—to help you parent your children. With practice, you will know which ones work best for you, and you may even modify them to fit your personality. You will find that having skill will create an inner peacefulness for you. You will find that having choices and plans in advance will enable you to parent less through *emotion* and more through *decision*.

Avoid These Common Mistakes

Even the best parents make mistakes. Any one single mistake, over time, will not affect your total parenting effort. However, a specific mistake, repeated over and over, can make it tough for you to produce consistent results with your children. Take a moment to think about your parenting skills and learn how to make some changes.

Giving In

You say *No.* Your child asks why. You explain. Your child asks again. You say *No.* Your child pleads. You say *No.* Your child begs. You say *No.* Your child negotiates. You say *Yes.* (Remember Little Miss Shoes in the park?) Often a parent starts off on the right track, but children can wear down even the firmest parental intentions. Make yourself a promise in two parts:

1. Think before you say *Yes* or *No.*

2. When you say *No,* stick with it—even if you change your mind!

Children learn very quickly whether a parent can be convinced to change a decision. Once they have this figured out in the affirmative, you will never have peace again! It's much safer for you to take a moment to *think* before you say *Yes* or *No,* so that you can be prepared to stand behind your decision. Parents tell me that just by making this promise to themselves, it becomes easier to stick to their *No* when they say it.

I remember one day when I was leaving the house to run some errands—my mom was at home. Vanessa and David (then four and two) asked if they could go with me. I said, "No, not now." They said, "Please!" I said, "No." Then they did something that would wear down even the hardest of hearts: each took an end of my dress and clung onto it. With tears welling in her eyes, Vanessa said, "I love you so much, Mommy. Please take me with you. I'll even put on my own seat belt. I'll do everything you say." David, in tears, said, "Me too! I'll be *so* good." At this point I realized that I should have said yes. I was in no hurry, and it would really be okay to take them.

However, I just said *No*—twice. If I changed my mind and said *Yes,* I would just be *teaching them* to cling and cry and plead whenever they wanted something from me. So I left them crying at the door, drove to the mailbox at the corner, and mailed a letter—turned around, and came back to the house, walked inside, and said, "Hi! I'm back! I have another errand to run, do you guys want to go with me?" Talk about a creative way to stick to your *No* guns!

There Is a Time for Compromise, Too

Now that I've got your promise to stick with a *No* when you say it, I'm going to turn around and tell you that there are times when it's okay to change your mind. You need to know your children and yourself enough to know when to allow for flexibility and compromise. These traits are important to teach your children, and, as with most values and skills, they are best taught by modeling. It's important that you *choose* to be flexible, as opposed to being *pushed into compromise* by a whining, nagging, pleading child. There is a big difference. Here's an example:

Inappropriate Compromise

Jim:	Can I go to Nathan's?
Father:	No. Not today.
Jim:	Why not? You never let me go anywhere!
Father:	I said *No!*
Jim:	But Dad, Ryan and Josh are going!
Father:	Jim, quit nagging me.
Jim:	I promise I'll be home by dinnertime! Really!
Father:	Well, okay. But you better be home by dinnertime!

Appropriate Compromise

Jim:	Can I go to Nathan's?
Father:	No. Not today.
Jim:	But Dad, Ryan and Josh are going!
Father:	Are they visiting their dad again? I know you three hardly get to see each other anymore. Just make sure you're home by dinnertime.
Jim:	Gee, thanks, Dad! I will.

By being fair and flexible, you model important life skills to your children. By allowing your children to use valid reasons to encourage you to change a decision, you demonstrate that their feelings and needs are important. Your children also learn that Mom and Dad are not perfect human beings, which allows you some slack to make mistakes sometimes.

Fuzzy Expectations

Kids and parents may attach wildly different definitions to the same concepts. For example, when you say, "Clean your room," you mean, "Put your toys away, hang up your clothes, make the bed, throw away garbage, vacuum." When your child hears "Clean your room," he thinks, "Pile everything in the closet or under the bed." Sometimes, of course, your child knows full well what you mean but *pretends* not to. In either case, giving clear instructions will allow your child to know *exactly* what you expect. One of two things will then happen: either he'll do it; or he won't, but because you know that he understood the statement, you can discipline him accordingly.

> Noreen, mother of Ryan, age eight, best friend to another eight-year-old Ryan (she calls them Ryan Squared), uses this principle beautifully whenever they go out to eat at a restaurant. In the car, in the parking lot, she pulls out a notepad from the glove compartment. On it is a list titled "Restaurant Manners." She reads, "Okay, Ryan Squared, remember your restaurant manners. One. Sit in your seat. Two. Quiet, inside voices. Three. No throwing food. Four. Use your silverware. Five. No fighting." If a rule is broken once they are in the restaurant, she simply reminds them by using the shorthand phrase, "Restaurant Manners!"

Take a look at these examples of fuzzy versus clear expectations:

Fuzzy	Clear
Be good.	Sit in your chair quietly.
Clean your room.	Books on the shelf, toys in the toybox, clothes in the closet.

Share.	Take turns nicely without fighting
You know better!	I expect you to ask first.
Time to go.	Shoes and coat on, get in the car.
What do you say?	You need to say, "Please."
Jessica!	Jessica, please come to the kitchen.
Jessica!	Stop that loud noise.
Jessica!	Be gentle with the cat.
Jessica!	Watch it, you're spilling your milk!
Jessica!	Come here, right now.

Being more specific with your statements will leave less room for confusion and misunderstanding. It will allow you to remain in control of the situation. In addition, making a clear statement will keep your emotions under control because you will be focused on the situation and your words will address the situation as well. Misunderstanding and flared tempers will rule when a parent makes a fuzzy, general comment or request that focuses on the *child* rather than the situation, as in the examples above. *Be good! You know better!* or *Jessica!* give the message that the child is bad, rather than focusing on the child's bad behavior. You want to give the message that your child has a problem, or is exhibiting a problem behavior, but that there are available solutions. Stating your expectation in a clear, uncluttered way will accomplish this goal.

Allowing Bad Manners

Most parents insist on good manners from their children in public places or when visiting with friends. But many parents don't even recognize the bad manners their children use at home. You need to take the time to be more aware of the conversation occurring at home. It is easier to demand good manners when you model them yourself. So often I hear parents and children talking to each other without the courtesy they show even to strangers.

Bad manners—parent to child. I was standing in the elevator at the shopping mall with three other people when the doors opened and in walked a woman and her ten-year-old son. She pressed a floor button, and then her son began pressing several floor buttons at once. The mother smacked her son's hand, and said, "What's the matter with you? Stop pressing those buttons!" The boy turned bright red, and began staring at his shoes. The woman looked at me and said, "Kids these days can't seem to mind their manners."

It struck me that if I were to push several buttons, the woman probably would have said to me, "Can I help you figure out where you want to go?"

or some such polite remark. I know she would never have shown me the disrespect she had just displayed to her own flesh and blood. She seemed to be ruled by her embarrassment at her son's behavior to the point of forgetting her own manners.

Bad manners—child to parent. Here are two examples:

> Jack sits down to dinner and takes one look at his plate. He doesn't have a clue what's on it, but its very lack of familiarity makes it suspect in his mind. He looks up at his father and says, "Yuk. I'm not gonna eat this stuff. I want a hamburger."

> Molly walks in the door after her first day at baseball practice. Her mother asks, "How was the new coach, honey?" Molly says, "Huh?" Mom repeats, "How was the new coach?" to which Molly answers, "Okay. Ma, you need to get me a new mitt. Mine doesn't fit anymore."

You can encourage good manners at home by gently reminding your children of the correct way to speak to you or each other, and by modeling good manners yourself. Not only will you create a more respectful atmosphere at home, you will be teaching your child social skills that are vital to his success in the outside world.

Bad Manners (Child)	Good Manners (Child)
I want some milk.	May I please have a glass of milk?
Ugh. I hate peas.	I don't care for peas.
I need the salt.	Please pass the salt.
Yeah.	Yes, please.
Uh-uh.	No, thank you.
Huh?	Pardon me?
Move out of the way.	Excuse me.
You need to get me a new mitt.	Mom, my old mitt doesn't fit anymore. May I get a new one?

Bad Manners (Parent)	Good Manners (Parent)
Get me a hammer.	Will you please get me a hammer?
Don't talk to me that way!	What I would like to hear is, "Please may I have my dinner now?"
Don't touch that!	Please keep your hands to yourself.

What do you mean, I *need* to get you a new mitt. I don't *have to* get you anything, young lady!

What I would like to hear is, "Mom, my old mitt doesn't fit anymore. May I get a new one?"

Being Inconsistent—Consistently

"Children are unpredictable," writes Franklin P. Jones. "You never know what inconsistency they're going to catch you in next." I'm sure that Mr. Jones, quoted in *The Funny Side of Parenthood* (Simon and Schuster, 1994), was a parent at the time—because it takes one to know one. Of course, it's okay to bend the rules now and again. It's even okay to change your mind from a *No* to a *Yes* once in a while. However, problems arise when inconsistency is the *rule* rather than the *exception*.

In the Harris household, inconsistency is the norm. Mom and Dad Harris rule the roost through trial and error—every day. Emotions typically run high, and the kids, Kyle and Matthew, don't have a clue as to what's expected of them. On Saturday, everyone was in a good mood. The kids took the cushions off every piece of furniture around, and built a great fort. Mom even served them lunch in the fort. When Kyle ran in to tell his mom that Matthew hit him and took his toy, she sent Matthew to his room and gave Kyle his toy. Later that night, the boys ate snacks as they watched a movie late into the night, and fell asleep on the family room floor in their clothes.

A few days later, the kids built another fort. When Mom walked in the door from work, she took one look at the fort and screamed, "Look at this mess! How am I supposed to clean the house and make dinner and go to work when you kids are always creating a disaster? Clean this stuff up right now!" The boys shrugged their shoulders and cleaned up. When Kyle ran in to tell his Mom that Matthew hit him and took his toy, she snapped, "Well, go work it out with your brother." Later, when they were snacking and watching a movie, Dad stormed in and yelled, "You guys are getting pizza all over the carpet! If you're gonna have a snack, eat in the kitchen!"

At bedtime, the boys brought their sleeping bags into the family room and got ready to settle down for the night. Mom, however, had other ideas. "What's wrong with you kids? Put these sleeping bags away, get your pajamas on, and get in bed."

Mom Harris later said to her husband, "I don't know what's wrong with these boys. They're always pulling something, and they never listen!" Dad responded, "Yeah. It's just kids these days. They never follow the rules."

Kyle and Matthew, in the meantime, are struggling to figure out just what the rules are!

When parents are inconsistent, children will test the rules constantly. It is very much like the gambler who plays the slot machines. A gambler will put money into a machine only so many times with no return. If he hits the jackpot every 10 or 15 times, the gambler will stick like glue to that machine. However, if after 30 or 40 tries there is still no reward, the gambler will find a new game. Keep this in mind when disciplining your children. It's okay to be inconsistent once in a while. But if your little gambler knows that it's possible at any moment to win the game, he'll pull that lever every time.

What helps a parent stay consistent? **Well-thought-out rules, routines, and the use of skills keep parents consistent in their everyday interactions with their children.**

To Sum Up

In this book we will help you create your own family rules, routines, and methods of discipline. Once you have rules—and once your children know what the rules are, and what the consequences are for breaking them—your household will run more smoothly. You will be calmer and more in control because you will have a plan. And you will be more able to handle the every-day issues and problems of parenting with a cool, level head.

Reminder Page—
The Keys to Successful Parenting

Take Charge

Expect your children to obey. No guilt, no excuses.

Think

Have a parenting plan.

When You Say It, Mean It

Think. Warn. Act. Follow through.

Use Skill

What is the goal? What skill will help me achieve my goal?

Avoid These Mistakes

- Giving in
- Having fuzzy expectations
- Allowing bad manners
- Being inconsistent

3

Cooperation

How Can You Get Kids to Do What You Want Them to Do When You Want Them to Do It

What can disrupt the peace and harmony in your home more than anything else? What can turn a routine activity into a full-scale battle? What can turn a normal parent into a screaming lunatic? A child who refuses to cooperate.

Throughout the course of a day, a week, a month, or a year—until your children grow up and leave home—you must somehow get them to do the things that must be done. It can sometimes seem that you're barking orders at your kids all day long: get up, get dressed, eat breakfast, get on the bus, go to school, play nicely, share, clean your room, feed your pet, put the milk away, close the door—and on and on and on. And to complicate matters, kids rarely do something the first time they are asked. So then *you* sound like a broken record, or a blasting boombox.

Would you like to know how to get your children to willingly cooperate? Would you like to eliminate many of your daily battles? Would it be even better if during the process you could teach your kids valuable life skills? If you're a parent, I'm sure your answer is *Yes, Yes,* and *Yes!* But before we look at the positive ways to encourage your children's cooperation, let's examine the methods parents usually employ.

During a typical day, a parent may resort to many methods to encourage a child to cooperate, many of them involving negative communication. Let's take a look at some of the ways in which parents try to enlist their children's cooperation.

Nagging

Parent:	John, you need to take out the trash.
(Later):	Don't forget to take out the trash.
(Later):	This trash is getting in my way. I wish you'd take it out.
(Later):	John, are you going to take out this trash?
(Later):	Are you ever going to take out this trash?

Wishing/Hoping

Parent: I don't think you should be up there with your roller-blades on. I sure wish you'd come down.

Pleading/Begging/Whining

Parent: Will you kids *please* stop fighting? I hate it when you act like this. Would you just be nice to each other until we get home? I don't know why I take you with me. Just be nice for a while!

Bribing

Parent: If you get in the car right now, I'll give you a cookie!

Empty Threats

Parent: Stop that right now or I'll never take you to McDonald's again!

Demands

Parent: Get off the sofa this minute!

Expressing Disgust

Parent: How many times do I have to tell you to keep your feet off the table? You never listen. What are you—a pig?

Lectures

Parent: That's the third jacket you've lost! You need to take more responsibility for your things. When I buy you a jacket, I expect it to last more than a week. If you would be more careful, and not leave it lying around, then you wouldn't lose it. I'm going to buy you one more jacket, but I don't want you to lose this one!

Yelling

Parent: Get in here right now! When I call you I expect you to come!

The similar thing about all these methods to enlist children's cooperation is that they often don't work at all. They also play a major role in creating an atmosphere of anger, resentment, and anxiety in the family. Parents become frustrated and angry over their children's lack of cooperation, and children become angry over the methods by which their parents attempt to "control them" (in the words of one adolescent).

The other problem with many of these methods is that they *are sometimes* effective in the short term, misleading parents into thinking that everything is going well. For example, a parent who rules with an iron fist may have children who are very "well-behaved"—in other words, they come when called, are quiet and respectful, and listen to the parent. But in reality these children are behaving out of fear of the parent or fear of punishment. They are not learning the inner discipline they will need in their lives to control their own behavior. They are not learning the necessary skills to develop self-control, responsibility, and decision making. Often these children will misbehave behind their parents' back, if they think they can get away with it. Look out when such children reach adolescence! That's when they cannot be controlled by the threats, punishments, and demands that worked when the children were younger. They often decide that a given misbehavior is worth the punishment, since the punishment is seen as the ultimate end to the issue. They do not understand the long-term consequences of their behavior, because they have not experienced it for themselves. For example, an adolescent concerned about driving too fast for fear of wrecking the car and getting Dad angry is far more likely to break the speed limit and endanger himself and others than an adolescent who understands that the consequences of speeding involve life and death and the possibility of getting a ticket that he or she will personally have to deal with.

There are a multitude of ways to encourage your children's cooperation without having to resort to yelling, bribing, threatening, and nagging. Let's examine some options that not only maintain the love in your relationship with your child, but also result in cooperation while helping children develop long-term self-discipline and decision-making skills.

Make a Statement

Unknowingly, parents often treat children as if they were completely inept, or incapable of understanding what is said to them. Instead of communicating clearly and directly, parents analyze, blame, accuse, or use sarcasm as a way to express their disapproval and in a roundabout effort to get children to cooperate. In this way, parents add a lot of emotional baggage to a simple statement, and turn it into a call for battle.

Mrs. Fernandez walks into the living room. The coffee table is littered with the remains of take-out food containers, candy wrappers, and half-eaten food. Meanwhile, her 14-year-old son is in front of the TV and VCR, playing a video game, completely oblivious to the mess he's made. His mom throws up her hands and says, "Why am I cursed with such a child?"

Jerome has been asked twice to take out the trash. As his father picks up some of the overflow from the kitchen floor and stuffs it into the trash can, he says to his son, "Have you taken out that trash yet?"

Sally's dog is whining desperately by the door to go out. Sally's mother says, "Do you want that dog to pee all over the carpet?"

Mrs. Taylor walks into the den to see Mark's new set of paints and brushes scattered all over the desk. Several of the bottles of paint are open, and the brushes are unwashed. She yells across the house at her son, "Mark! You are so irresponsible! Get in here and clean up these paints and brushes! Look at this mess! I don't even know why I bother buying you such nice things!"

In each of these situations, the parent's dissatisfaction comes through loud and clear. But the underlying theme of each of these interchanges is the parent's communication that the child is "bad." Each presentation needs to be amended to include a *statement* free of blame or accusation. When you do this, you will demonstrate your respect for your child's intelligence. It will, in essence, change the underlying content of the conversation to: "You are a good kid, and you have a problem."

Let's revisit each of the previous situations, this time in a more positive way by simply "making a statement."

Mrs. Fernandez walks into the living room. The coffee table is littered with the remains of take-out food containers, candy wrappers, and half-eaten food. Meanwhile, her 14-year-old son is in front of the TV and VCR, playing a video game, completely oblivious to the mess he's made. His mom says, "Juan, I need you to listen to me for a moment. When you're done with the game, I want you to clean up the mess on the coffee table."

Jerome has been asked twice to take out the trash. As his father picks up some of the overflow from the kitchen floor and stuffs it into the trash can, he says to his son, "Jerome, the trash can is overflowing."

Sally's dog is desperately whining by the door to go out. Sally's mother says, "Blackie is waiting by the door for you to take her out."

Mrs. Taylor walks into the den to see Mark's new set of paints and brushes scattered all over the desk. Several of the bottles of paint are open, and the brushes are unwashed. She walks into the next room where Mark is reading a book, gets eye-to-eye with her son, and says, "Mark, your new paints and brushes need to be put away. They're getting all dried out. They're also making it impossible for anyone else to use the desk."

If any of these children do *not* complete the task at hand, the parent can then follow through with additional skills, or a change of tactics. When parents use a statement of fact, it takes all the fight out of the request, and enables children to cooperate while feeling good about themselves. Using a statement of fact allows children to take responsibility for their own behavior. It allows them to hear the fact, think about the information, and act accordingly. It is also much easier for children to follow their own logical conclusions than to second-guess their parents, or deal with negative emotions that only get in the way of cooperation.

Use Grandma's Rule

In my grandma's day, it was understood that children had certain responsibilities as members of the family. They "earned" their privileges by fulfilling their responsibilities first. The idea behind this rule is that you acknowledge something the child would *like* to do as the second step. You define the first step as a chore, action, or activity that must be done before the privilege is granted. The benefits to this approach are threefold. First, your request is very specific, and thus can be understood by your child. Second, you are acknowledging your child's wants and needs at the same time you are stating *your* wants and needs. Third, you are approaching the issue in a way that invites your child to cooperate. Here's how it works:

You may _____ **after you** _____ .

You may <u>play outside</u> after you <u>do the dishes.</u>

You may <u>watch a movie</u> after you <u>do your homework.</u>

We will <u>read a story</u> after you <u>put your pajamas on.</u>

Using Grandma's Rule eliminates the need to use "fighting words." Fighting words are those that start a battle even before the rest of the sentence is heard—words such as, *You can't, Don't, No,* and *Stop!*

Notice how the choice of words affects the feeling conveyed by these requests:

Fighting Words	Grandma's Rule
You can't go outside until you finish your homework.	You may go outside after you finish your homework.

Fighting Words	**Grandma's Rule**
Don't eat that cookie until after dinner.	You can eat that cookie right after dinner.
No, you can't go to Jimmy's house.	You can go to Jimmy's house on Saturday, after soccer practice.

Give Clear Instructions

Parents sometimes hint at what they want their child to do, rather than saying it outright. They use opening lines such as, *"I sure wish you'd ..."* or *"It would be nice if you ..."* or *"I think you should ..."* or *"I would really like it if you ..."* Such hints are veiled requests for action, but the way in which they are presented allows the child to interpret them as an option. Parents need to drop the questions, and make clear requests instead:

Veiled Requests	**Clear Requests**
I sure wish you'd get your pajamas on.	Please put your pajamas on.
It would be nice if you cleaned up your books.	Please clean up your books.
I think you should do your homework before you go out to play.	Please do your homework before you go out to play.

A second variation on this problem is an incomplete or "fuzzy" request. Children and parents can often interpret the same notion or phrase completely differently. Parents need to be perfectly clear when setting limits, requesting obedience, or asking for cooperation. When a fuzzy request is given, it can be unclear whether your child misunderstood you, or is simply defying you. When a clear request is given, your child *still* may not follow through, but you will at least be sure that he or she understood the request, and you can take appropriate action.

Fuzzy Request	**What the Child Hears**	**Clear Request**
Please clean up your room.	Put everything in the closet.	Please put your books on the shelf, your clothes in the closet, and your toys in the toy-box.
Time to go!	Time to think about getting ready to go.	Please put your shoes and coat on, and get in the car.

You know better!	You did something wrong.	I expect you to ask before taking out my scissors.
Jessica!	Hi, Jessica!	Jessica, please come to the kitchen!
Be good.	I notice you.	Sit in your chair. Use a quiet, inside voice.

Give a Choice

Giving a choice is a very powerful tool that can be used with toddlers through teenagers. This is one skill that every parent should have tattooed on the back of his or her hand as a constant reminder. Parents should use this skill every day, many times a day. Giving children choices is a very effective way to enlist their cooperation, because children love having the privilege of choice. It takes the pressure out of a request, and allows a child to feel in control. This makes a child more willing to comply.

Using choice is an effective way to achieve results while allowing your children to learn self-discipline, and develop good decision-making skills. When you get in the habit of offering choices many times each day, you are doing your children a big favor. As children learn to make simple choices—*Milk or juice?*—they get the practice required to make bigger choices—*Buy two class T-shirts, or one sweatshirt?*—which gives them the ability as they grow to make more important decisions—*Save or spend? Drink beer or soda? Study or fail?* Giving children choices allows them to learn to listen to their inner voice. It is a valuable skill which they will carry with them to adulthood.

There are several key points to remember when using choice.

Offer Choices Based on the Child's Age, and Your Intent

A toddler can handle two choices, a grade-school child three or four. A teenager can be given general guidelines. Remember to offer choices such that you would be happy with whatever option your child chooses. Otherwise, you're not being fair. For example, a parent might say, "Either eat your peas or go to your room"; but when the child gets up off his chair, the parent yells, "Sit down and eat your dinner, young man!" Another parent might ask his child, "What do you want for breakfast?"; and when the child says, "Spaghetti," the parent answers, "That's not a breakfast food. Pick something else."

Here are some ways in which you can use choice:

Do you want to wear your Big Bird pajamas, or your Mickey Mouse pajamas?

Do you want milk or orange juice?

Which pair of shorts would you like to wear today?

Do you want to do your homework at the kitchen table or the dining room table?

Do you want to wear your coat, carry it, or put on a sweatshirt?

Do you want to let the dog out in the yard or take him for a walk?

Use Time as a Choice

A wonderful way to use choice when there really is only one acceptable option is to offer a choice of *time* or *sequence*. This method keeps you in control of the outcome, while giving a child some flexibility in meeting your needs. Some examples of this:

Do you want to watch five more minutes of TV, or ten more minutes?

Shall I pick you up at Jennifer's before I shop or after?

What do you want to do first, take out the trash or feed the dog?

Do you want to put your shirt on first, or your pants?

Will you do your homework now, after dinner, or shall I wake you at six?

If Children Won't Choose, Make It Clear That They're Choosing Not to Choose

If a child is reluctant to choose from the options you offer, then simply ask, "Would you like to choose, or shall I choose for you?" If your child gets stubborn and refuses to choose, you can say, "I see that you want me to choose"—and then *follow through*. For example, if you are trying to get your preschooler out the door in the morning, and you ask, "Do you want to wear your shoes or your sneakers?" and he says, "I don't want to go," you can say, "I see that you want me to choose." Then *you* decide, put them on for him, and lead (or carry) him out the door (without nagging or yelling).

A typical problem with choices is the child who makes up his own choice. For example, "John, do you want to put on your pajamas first, or brush your teeth?" To which John replies, "I want to watch TV." You can then smile sweetly and say, "That wasn't one of the choices." Then smile again as you repeat, "Do you want to put on your pajamas first, or brush your teeth?"

A mother in one of my classes reported using this skill with great success at home. It was after dinner and she said to her *husband*, "Would you like to clean up the dishes, or put the kids to bed?" He said, "Hey! You're using that choice thing on me!" (All of the skills presented in this book work with adults, too.)

Different Children, Different Choices

When our daughter Vanessa was two, we noticed that there were times when having a choice would *not* make her grateful for the opportunity. Instead, it would throw her into a temper tantrum, and she would end up sobbing. We'd ask her if she wanted cereal or waffles for breakfast, and she'd demand toast, then reject the toast because I dared to cut it in *triangles!* So I'd make her some new toast, cut in perfect squares, and she'd collapse in tears because it had too much butter on it. Being a loving mommy, I'd try to scrape off the butter; but, as any respectable person should know, it's just not the same. Later that day, Vanessa would happily choose her jacket over her coat, her blocks over her puzzles, and her snack from a variety she was offered. What I came to realize was that Vanessa was just *not* a morning person. She woke up slowly, and would rather sit on the sofa and stare into space for a while than eat breakfast, let alone have to make all those decisions about breakfast. I realized that when it comes to giving choices, parents must carefully consider when, where, and how to offer them. Although it's vitally important for children to learn how to make choices, it helps to consider your child's personality, mood, and experience when offering the freedom to make decisions.

Parents need to know which decisions their children are ready to make, and which ones they're not ready for—regardless of what the children would *like* to do. To avoid frustration and battles of will while helping to build your child's decision-making skills, it's important to exercise some control over the choices being made available. Clearly, anything that could compromise your child's future, health, or safety is not for him or her to decide. Nor can you allow decisions that affect other people in overtly negative ways. However, there are a myriad of choices that can safely be made by any child. Offering choices is especially important when dealing with those issues over which you have little real control—what your children wear, what they eat, who their friends are, how quickly they fall asleep, and when they go potty.

Offering children choices is a peaceful way to encourage their cooperation while avoiding the power struggle that so often erupts when a parent gives an order. When you are careful and thoughtful about when and how to offer choices, and when you respect the choices your child makes, you are helping him or her develop important life skills. The added benefit is that when children choose their own plan of action, they are more likely to follow through with a pleasant attitude. So, do you want to start offering choices today or tomorrow?

Make It Brief

"How many times do I have to tell you to ask before you borrow my things! It's showing respect and good manners to ask first. I never take your things without asking, and I expect the same from you. Why do I always have to repeat myself? Now, look, this sweatshirt is dirty and I wanted to wear it today. Now I have to change my plans because ..."

Lectures, nagging, and long discussions cause many children to become "parent deaf." They seem to have selective hearing that turns off whenever a parental lecture is in session. A child will stand there and stare blankly at you while nodding and uh-huhing at the appropriate places, and then turn around and repeat the behavior that you were trying to change in the first place. Parents can avoid this cycle of wasted words and negative energy by keeping their comments brief and to the point.

A brief comment allows you to capture your child's attention, make your point, and give him or her the *responsibility* to follow through.

This is too long a statement, it seems to go on and on, your child will probably tune you out, the lesson you are trying to teach will not be learned, your voice will get tired, and ...	**Excellent choice!**
Your guinea pig doesn't have any water. It's very important that she always have water in her bottle. It seems like I'm always reminding you. I want you to be responsible for your pet, and make sure she has food and water every day. Now, will you please take care of her?	Ginger needs water.
Andrea! Why are you watching TV? You know the rule. Your homework has to be done before you can watch TV. We set up that rule because you were always forgetting your homework. It shouldn't be up to me to get you	Andrea, homework first!

motivated. I'd like you to take some responsibility. Now turn off that TV and go do your homework.

Kids! How many times do I have to tell you to put your toys away before dinner? You guys know the rule, yet every day you come to dinner and I see the family room littered with toys. Before I put any food on the table, I expect to see that room cleaned up.

Kids—the rule is, toys put away before dinner.

Make Something Talk

This tool is worth its weight in gold for the under-five age group. Preschoolers require finesse to gain their cooperation, because they have not yet reached the age at which they can see and understand the whole picture. Robert Scotellaro is quoted in *The Funny Side of Parenthood* as saying, "Reasoning with a two-year-old is about as productive as changing seats on the Titanic." (He must have had a two-year-old at the time!) You *can* get around this frustrating state of affairs by changing your approach. Making something talk is one great way to get a young child to listen to you and cooperate. Let's look at two situations—first, the typical (Titanic) way:

Parent:	David! Time to change your diaper.
David:	No! (As he runs off)
Parent:	Come on, honey. It's time to go, I need to change you.
David:	(Giggles and hides behind the sofa)
Parent:	David. This isn't funny. It's getting late. Come here.
David:	(Doesn't hear a word; sits down to do a puzzle)
Parent:	David, come here! We need to get ready to go! (Gets up and approaches David)
David:	(Giggles and runs)
Parent:	(Picking up David) Now lie here. Stop squirming! Lie still. Will you please stop this! (As parent turns to pick up a diaper, a little bare bottom is running in the opposite direction . . .)

I'm sure you've all been there (by the way, David is *my* son). Like you, I got very tired of chasing a toddler. And then I discovered a better way.

Parent: (Picking up diaper and holding it like a puppet, making it talk in a squeaky voice) Hi, David! I'm Dilly Diaper! Come here and play with me!

David: (Runs over to the diaper) Hi!

Parent
as Diaper: You're such a nice boy. Will you give me a kiss?

David: Yes. (Gives the diaper a kiss)

Parent
as Diaper: How about a nice hug?

David: (Giggles and hugs the diaper)

Parent
as Diaper: Lie right here on the floor, next to me, right here, yup. Can I go on you? Oh! Goody goody goody! (The diaper chats with David while he's being changed. Then it says—Oh, David! Listen, I hear your shoes calling you—David! David!

The most amazing thing about this trick is that it works over and over and over and over. You'll keep thinking, "He's not honestly going to fall for this *again!*" But he will! Probably the nicest by-product of this method is that it gets *you* in a good mood, and you have a little fun time with your child. (Remember—it only works if you use a special voice—squeaky, silly, appropriate for a puppet.) One day, when my son David was almost three, I was making my hand talk to him. He was hugging my hand, and looked up at me and said, "Mommy, I love you to pretend this hand is talking!" Another day, after I had called David to the table for dinner a number of times, he calmly looked up at me and said, "Mommy, why don't you just have my dinner call to me?"

Karen, mother to two-year-old Matthew, reported this story: At lunchtime she was trying to get Matthew to drink his milk. She reached over to the Mickey Mouse balloon that was attached to his chair, and said in a Mickey-like voice, "Matthew—drink your milk, it's good for you!" He said, "Okay, Mickey!" and did. Later that day, at dinnertime, Matthew pulled the balloon down to his level and said in a Mickey-like voice, "Hey, Mattchew, dink your mik, it's good for you!"

I have been delighted to discover that this technique works even for older children who know exactly what you're up to. Allison, mother of five-year-old Caitlin, shared this story with me:

I have used many of the skills I learned in your classes, but I never thought to "make something talk," because I figured that

Caitlin was too old for it. Well, was I wrong! Last night was bath night. Caitlin has long, thick hair, and hates to have it washed. Usually, bath time turns into a real battle, with Caitlin crying and me getting angry! Well, last night, just as I was about to wash her hair, and dreading it, I glanced over at a little plastic bear and thought, "Why not!?" I picked up the bear and *it* said, in a very "bear-y" voice, "Hi, Caitlin! Can I wash your hair tonight?" To my surprise, she said, "Yes!" and proceeded to cooperate with the bear. The kicker came when it was time to rinse, which is usually our real moment of battle. The bear asked, "How many times should I rinse your hair?" And Caitlin answered, "A thousand!" I couldn't believe it! Later, when she was all snug in her pajamas, I was giving her a hug and said, "Boy, does your hair smell pretty." She gave me a know-it-all look and said, "Mommy, that's 'cuz a *bear* washed it!"

A variation on this technique is to capitalize on a young child's vivid imagination as a way to thwart negative emotions. My husband Robert used this idea one sunny afternoon as we walked home from the park with our children. Vanessa was four years old at the time. I'll demonstrate two different ways of handling the situation. (Happily, the *second* scene is what really happened.)

Scene 1—What Could Have Happened

Vanessa: (Whining) I don't want to walk anymore.

Daddy: We're almost home.

Vanessa: But I'm tired. Carry me.

Daddy: You're too big to carry. It's just a little longer.

Vanessa: No! I'm tired. (Sits down on the sidewalk)

Daddy: Stop this and walk.

Vanessa: (Crumbles on the sidewalk and cries)

Scene 2—What Really Happened

Vanessa: (Whining) I don't want to walk anymore.

Daddy: I bet you wish a magic pony would appear and you could ride him home!

Vanessa: A pony with wings! And I could fly home.

Daddy: Two ponies! One for me, too!

Vanessa:	Mine would be green and yours would be red, and the wings would have every color on them.
Angela:	I want one, too! Mine would fly to the tops of the houses.
David:	(Begins to gallop down the sidewalk. Vanessa, Daddy, and Angela follow suit.)

It's delightful to see how a potentially negative situation can be turned into a fun experience by changing a child's focus to fantasy.

5–3–1–Go!

Go with me now to an indoor kid park with all sorts of wonderful activities and equipment for young children. Let's look in at the play area and watch as various parents try to encourage their children to put on their shoes and leave for home:

"Becky, time to go!" says Nellie Nag. It appears that Becky has not heard her, so Nellie repeats herself, "Becky! Time to go." Becky continues to play with her new friend, Peter. But Peter's mom, Betty Briber, is whispering in his ear, "If you get in the car right now, I'll buy you a box of those cute little cookies you like, and you can eat them on the way home!" Meanwhile, Letty Lecture is looking up the slide at her two kids and saying, "You know, guys, when I take you to this place, I expect you to cooperate when it's time to go. I bring you here because I know you love it. But when I ask you to put your shoes on, I would like you to listen. Last time we came here .... " Nellie's voice can still be heard over the din: "Becky. It's time to put your shoes on, honey." Meanwhile, Wishy Wanda can be heard wondering about her children's behavior: "I sure wish you kids would put your shoes on. It would be nice if you listened to me." Oh, and in the background: "Becky, don't you have your shoes on yet?" Everyone pauses for a minute as Bret Threat shouts, "Get in that car right now or I'll never let you come here again!" Bret's children hurry out to the car, as they pass Count Casey and hear him say, "If you kids aren't in the car by the time I count to three . . ."

"Becky! Find your shoes, and let's get going," says Nellie Nag. In the meantime, Wilma Whiner sounds like fingernails on a blackboard: "Kiiiids. Come ooooon. I asked you to put your shoooes ooooon. Will you pleeeeeze listen to meeeee." But her kids aren't really listening to her, because they are busy playing with Becky . . .

Sound familiar? Just listen in on any birthday party, neighborhood park, or gymnastics class, and you'll hear all these parents trying to gain their children's attention and cooperation. So, you want to know, just how *do* you get them to leave the kid park?

First, let's try to understand what's going on here. When kids are having a good time, it's hard for them to change gears on a dime, which is what we expect. When a kid is in the middle of a great game with a new friend, and Dad walks in and says, "Time to go," it's hard for a child to immediately comply. Actually, it's hard for *adults* to do this too. Picture yourself at the computer typing away when your spouse calls, "Honey, dinner's ready!" Do you immediately pop off your chair and run to the kitchen? Or do you answer back, "Just a minute," and take the time to finish your paragraph, save your work, tidy up your desk, and—only then—saunter into the kitchen?

What really helps children prepare to finish or change activities is to allow them the time to process the change *mentally* before they follow through *physically*. Watch how this happens:

> Molly and Austin are happily playing together at the park while Mom is reading on a nearby bench. She looks up at them and says, "Molly! Austin! We're leaving in five minutes," she holds up five very visible fingers. Somewhere in the back of Molly's and Austin's minds the information is filtering through. A few minutes later, Mom says, "Molly! Austin! We're leaving in three minutes." She holds up three fingers. A few minutes later: "Molly! Austin! One minute! Do you want to have one more swing or one more slide?" "Slide!" they shout. After the slide, Mom says, "Time to go. You guys want to run to the car, or hop like bunnies?" And the three of them hop to the car.

A few pointers on 5-3-1-Go! You can adjust this technique to meet your family's needs, your children's ages, or your personality. For instance, for a 16-year-old, you may pop your head in the family room as she's watching TV and say, "Corine, we're leaving at 3:00 sharp. It's 2:45 now." You can use this technique to call your kids to dinner, to the bathtub, or to bed. Keep in mind one very important point: this won't work the first time you use it. And probably not the second. But, by about the third or fourth time, your kids will understand and accept this new way of doing things. From the first, when you say, "Time to go!" you *must immediately go*. If you don't, this won't be any different from any of the old techniques that don't work.

> A student named Mel called to tell me about trying this technique. In a rather grim voice, he told me, "It better work."
> "You sound angry," I said. "Oh, yes. I took my four-year-old to

McDonald's. I said, 'Matthew, five minutes ... three minutes ... one minute ... time to go!' And he jumped into the ball pit. So, I remembered what you said about meaning business when you say *Go*; and I jumped in the ball pit after him! Do you know how hard it is to get out of one of those things with a screaming, kicking four-year-old under your arm? (I felt like selling tickets!)

The good news is that, yes, indeed, Mel did stick with the idea, and a few months later reported that it was working like a charm.

Ask Helpful Questions

You can help your children learn to listen to their inner voice and help them develop self-discipline by asking helpful questions. The goal here is to keep your emotions out of the way, and assist your children in thinking through their problems and arriving at their own solutions. Parents often ask their children questions, but they are usually far from helpful:

Why did you do that?

How many times do I have to tell you?

What is wrong with you?

Such questions only block your child's thinking process, and do nothing to help solve the problem. But helpful questions, presented in a thoughtful manner, can point your child toward a solution or mitigation of the problem. Here are some examples of questions that can be used in a variety of situations to help your child develop constructive problem-solving skills:

How do you feel about that?

Can you think of some ways we might solve this problem together?

How do you think your brother feels about this?

Are you happy about what you made happen?

How could you have handled that differently?

What will you do now?

I was delighted to witness the following scene between my children, David, age three, and Vanessa, age five. I had just given David a handful of jelly beans to share with his sister. As they sat on the floor together, I heard Vanessa say to David, "You have seven and I have only three. Do you think that's fair?" To which David replied, "No, I don't. But that's okay, I'll give you some more." Helpful question. Thoughtful answer.

The key to making these questions work is to keep your emotions out of it, so that your child can focus on the question and the solution without worrying about *your* involvement in the problem, or *your* anger. I have heard more than one parent of a teenager complain that their child never talks to them about anything, but spends an hour talking nonstop to the school counselor. The difference is clearly that a counselor has been taught to ask helpful questions, in a nonthreatening way, and then to *listen* to the child's answers and direct him through his own thinking process.

The following scenes demonstrate the pleasant difference that can occur when helpful questions are used. Try to imagine what Nancy's feelings and responses would be after each scene.

Thirteen-year-old Nancy wore her sister's sweatshirt without permission, and stained the front of it with purple marker. Her mom discovered this and....

Scene 1 ... stormed into her room, yelling, "Nancy! What is the matter with you? You know the rules!! Why did you take Amy's shirt without asking? Look at this, it's ruined! Young lady, you are grounded for a week, and we'll cover the cost of a new shirt out of tomorrow's allowance."

What do you think Nancy's response would be?

How do you think Nancy feels about her mother now?

How do you think Nancy feels about *herself* now?

How do you think Nancy feels about *Amy* after this exchange?

Scene 2 ... walked into her room and sat on her bed.

Mom:	Nancy, how do you think Amy will feel when she sees her sweatshirt?
Nancy:	She's gonna be mad.
Mom:	I think so. How do you think you should handle this?
Nancy:	I don't know ... I guess I could give her one of my sweatshirts. Maybe the green one that she really likes. Do you think that's okay?

How do you think Nancy feels about her mother now?

How do you think Nancy feels about *herself* now?

How do you think Nancy feels about *Amy* after this exchange?

It's easy to see that helpful questions delivered in a calm, respectful way can help lead your children to find their own answers. It also gives them a feeling of being loved and respected, and will draw them closer to you. In his sensitive book, *The Ten Greatest Gifts I Give My Children*, author Steven Vannoy says, "If you think it's difficult to find the time to listen now, I assure you that the pain of being cut off from the essence of those beautiful children when they stop talking to you will make you wish you'd found the time or the willingness to listen earlier."

Put It on Paper

Notes, lists, and drawings are a great way to communicate with your child and gain cooperation. Putting it down on paper is an effective way to communicate to children of all ages. The written word has a way of carrying a silent power that effectively encourages children to cooperate.

Seven-year-old Annie had a bad habit of totally neglecting her pet cat. She always claimed to forget to feed her and change her litter box. She and her mother got into an argument about this at bedtime most nights. No one liked the negative energy this topic was causing in the family. Today, Annie's mother tried something new. She wrote a note that said: *"Please take care of me before you go to bed! Meow!"* Mom taped the note to the bedroom door. It served as a quiet reminder to Annie, who liked the idea very much, since she didn't have to listen to her mother nag her.

Notes can also be very effective during a time when your angry emotions are running high. At such times, a note serves two functions. It puts space between you and your child, and it communicates your needs without turning up the volume. Typically, a note written in anger will be redone several times before it is delivered. Just the act of working out your emotions on paper releases a lot of angry tension. Also, a note has the potential to be clear and understandable, and can prevent miscommunication on important issues.

Believe it or not, even kids who can't read yet love notes! As a matter of fact, notes can be most effective with children from about age three to five, because during this time they are just starting to understand what reading and words are all about. Any note written to them will get their attention totally, quickly, and completely. (Just be prepared to read the note over and over and over again!) To give added emphasis to your message, and make it more fun, too, try sending it through the mail on a picture postcard. Kids love getting letters, especially if they're allowed to gather the mail themselves. Don't forget that you can also send loving messages along with lessons or reminders.

For the preschool set, you can post a picture (such as a cutout from a magazine showing a child brushing her teeth) in a conspicuous place (such as on the pajama drawer). These pictures can serve as a reminder to you, your spouse, or the babysitter as well.

Use Humor

It's okay not to be serious all the time! Humor can get a child motivated to go along with you, and it keeps you in an upbeat frame of mind. It helps your children see the lighter side of life, and shows them that making a mistake is not fatal. Adding humor to your life helps you keep in perspective what's important and what's not. Humor increases the positive energy in your home, and draws the family closer together.

Remember to use respectful humor. Making fun of someone, teasing, or causing embarrassment is typically not seen as funny to a child, and can injure their fragile self-esteem.

There are so many ways to add humor to your interactions with your children. You just need to be more aware that humor is an option. Try telling the kid who is reluctant to take out the trash that there's an article about him in today's paper. Pretend to read about how your child was interviewed, and quote him saying how much he loves to take out the trash. Read how he won a gold medal for being the fastest person in the trash-carrying event at the Olympics. Then offer to time him.

Try singing a silly song to remind your children to get ready for bed (to the tune of "Jingle Bells"): *Hey there, kids. Time for bed. Time to brush your teeth. Oh, what fun it is to get your warm pajamas on! Ohhhhh. Hey there, kids. Time for bed* . . .

Most children prefer being joked with versus being nagged or yelled at. An added benefit is that you will find yourself lightening up.

Be careful, though. I used humor one day to diffuse the tension between Angela and Vanessa. The girls were sitting at the dinner table, and Vanessa was playing out the role of "pesky little sister," poking and pestering Angela. Angela complained to me that she tried talking to her, but it didn't help; she tried moving her seat, but Vanessa followed her. In my effort to lighten things up, I said to Angela, "Well, then, punch her in the nose!". . . and she did! (That's the last time I tried *that* joke.)

Use Rules and Routines

Family rules and routines organize your life. They are clear reminders to children to do what needs to be done without your having to constantly give orders. I always marvel at the parent of a 14-year-old who comes to me complaining about getting the child to do his homework. I mean, hasn't this parent already had seven *years* of homework to deal with? Or the parent of a six-year-old with a bedtime problem—how many nights does the child go to bed? Every night for the past six years, right? What's missing in each of these cases is a specific rule and routine for an everyday issue. Rules and routines can create more peace in a home than almost anything else I can think of.

Rules and routines are especially effective when prepared with time and thought, and when written down.

Good rules meet these requirements:

1. Make Rules in Advance

Don't invent your rules on the run. That isn't organization—it's disorganization, and it creates confusion. Take the time to sit down and think about what it is you expect from your children. Write the rules down. Update them every so often. Post them where everyone can see them as a gentle reminder of what needs to be done.

2. Make Rules You Can and Will Enforce

There is a rule about rules: when they are made, children will break them! Be prepared to handle this. Make your life easier by having fewer but more important rules. If you have too many rules, or rules that are too strict, you make it hard on yourself, since you constantly have to police your kids' activities, or else let broken rules slide by. Fewer but better rules make it easier for you to follow through. For example, perhaps you would like the kids to hang up their jackets when they walk in the door, and sometimes they do, sometimes they don't, sometimes you remind them, sometimes you do it yourself, and sometimes you just step over them because you don't feel like dealing with them. Understand that this should not be a "rule" (it can be "something I'd really like" instead).

3. State Rules Clearly, Keep Them Simple

Make sure that everyone understands the rules. Use fewer words to describe each rule. Use statements that cover a variety of things. As an example: "No hitting, biting, pushing, kicking, pulling hair, poking, shoving, or spitting" will only get you into trouble, because it's just too much to remember. Or your child may scratch her sister and then say, "But it's not on the list!" Better that the rule should say: "No hurting each other."

4. Plan Consequences for Breaking the Rules

When you decide what consequence or disciplinary action will occur when a rule is broken, it prevents your children from trying to negotiate with you about consequences. It also spells out the details for everyone, and gives you a plan to lean on when misbehavior occurs. Having the consequences known by all in advance can lessen the arguments that so often occur when discipline is necessary. The written rules become "boss," and this takes the burden of being the "bad guy" off the parents' shoulders.

Here's an example of one family's rules poster:

Our Family Rules

Rule	Consequence
1. No hurting each other.	Time out for five minutes, followed by apology. Must do one chore for the person who was hurt.
2. Homework done before dinner.	No outside play after dinner, stay in to do homework.
3. Chores done before bedtime.	Must do next morning before school. (Parent will wake you up early.)
4. No sassing, whining, or nagging.	Go immediately to your room, end of the discussion.

To Sum Up

You now have eleven new ideas for encouraging your child's cooperation. Try all the ideas and keep the ones that work for you. At first, the skills may feel awkward or strange—stick with it! You will become more comfortable with each skill as you practice it. Practice, patience, and persistence are required to change habits and improve your parenting style. Remember, every family is different, every child is different, and every situation is different. Be flexible and you may even invent some of your own ideas! Using "skill" to encourage your children's cooperation will make your life more peaceful and your parenting more fun.

Reminder Page—Cooperation

Make a Statement

The trash is overflowing. The dog wants to go out. Your crayons are on the floor.

Use Grandma's Rule

You may _____ after you _____ .
You may play outside after you do the dishes.

Give Clear Instructions

Please _____ (be specific).
Please put your shoes and coat on, and get in the car.

Give a Choice

This or that? Then or now? Me or you? Do you want milk or juice? Will you do your homework now or after dinner?

Make It Brief

Ginger needs water. Homework first! Toys!

Make Something Talk

Be creative. Use your funny puppet voice.

5–3–1–Go!

Be consistent. When you say *Go*, mean it!

Ask Helpful Questions

What will you do now? How can we solve this?

Put It on Paper

Use notes, lists, or drawings.

Use Humor

Make a joke, sing a song. Pick your battles wisely.

Use Rules and Routines

Make clear, simple rules you *will* enforce. Post them.

4

Punishment Versus Discipline

How were you punished as a child? When I ask this question in my classes, people pause for a few minutes, and I can tell they are thinking back to their childhood. Suddenly everyone begins to talk at once:

I was sent to my room without dinner, so I could "think" about it.

I was belittled until I felt stupid and inept.

I was spanked, slapped, pushed, or grabbed.

I was threatened and warned.

I had my most prized privileges taken away.

I was yelled at and lectured to.

In my house, my father had a belt hanging on a hook in the kitchen. It was a visible reminder to be good or be put over his knee. We were all afraid of that belt. One day, my father couldn't find it. Eventually it was found in the trash can, my little sister—then age six—had decided it would be a better place for it! (She was due for a spanking, and was trying to avoid it.) Once discovered, she knew her spanking would be worse than ever. When my father put her over his knee, he noticed that her little rear end had been replaced by a large lumpy surface—wadded-up handtowels in her underpants! He pulled out the handtowels, pulled down her underpants, and proceeded to hit her. I can still remember the welts on her bottom after her bare skin was hit with that belt. I remember thinking, "Yuk!" As a mother with three children of my own, the memory brings tears to my eyes. The odd thing about this story is that both my sister and I remember the spanking; but neither of us can recall what the misbehavior was that caused it. We know that our father must have been trying to teach us a lesson. The lesson, however, has been lost. The memory of the spanking is all that remains.

Our parents punished us, most likely, the same way in which they were punished. And *their* parents punished them the same way in which our grandparents were punished as children. After all, we learn what we live. We tend to parent the way we were parented, whether right or wrong. We may not even think about it, let alone question it.

Let's look at this pattern. Just because *it's always been done this way* does not always make it *the right way*. I can better illustrate my point through a story:

> Sally's mom was making a pot roast. As usual, she prepared the meat by cutting two inches off each end of the meat. Sally asked, "Why do you do that?" To which her mom replied, "I don't know. That's how *my* mother always did it." Sally, an ever-curious child, asked if she could call her grandmother to ask her why. When Grandma was asked the question, she replied, "I don't know. That's how *my* mother always did it." Sally, pressing to the end, asked if she could make the long-distance call to her great-grandmother. Sally asked her, "Why do you always cut off the ends of the pot roast before you cook it?" To which Great-Grandma replied, "Because it's too big to fit in my pan!"

As parents, we may need to periodically re-evaluate our child-rearing methods, especially checking for those destructive practices we may be following simply out of habit. We need to research the current data, analyze our current results, and continually look for the right answers. It always amazes me that people take classes to help them with all sorts of skills in their lives—skiing, exercising, driving, sewing, operating their computer. But when it comes to raising their children, they "play it by ear." Raising children is the most important job you will ever have. There are numerous books, articles, and classes available for parents. There are so many people you can learn from. Child psychologists, teachers, counselors, and other parents have blazed the trail before you, and are there to share wonderful skills, ideas, and methods that can be easily applied to your own situation. All parents need to take advantage of this knowledge in their quest to do the best job they can raising their children.

Why Do We Punish Our Children?

As caring, loving parents, we take the raising of our children seriously. We often think about the long-term results of what we are doing with our children today. A typical comment from parents who see a wild, out-of-control three-year-old is "He's going to be a handful when he's seven years old!" We acknowledge that the road a child is on, even as a toddler, can set him up for troublesome behavior patterns as he gets older. This is so very true! A child who has received little discipline in the younger years will not suddenly transform into an angel when he turns seven! Instead, things will usually go from bad to worse, and from worse to impossible. As parents, then, we punish our children *today* to have a better *tomorrow*. Following are some of the reasons why we punish our children.

1. To Stop Misbehavior

The first and most basic reason we punish is to stop misbehavior. We see a child breaking a rule or hurting another child, and our first instinct is to put a stop to the action. As good parents, we try to stop behavior problems *when they occur*. Often, this kind of punishment is more a "reflex" action:

Mary reports this story:

I walked into the room to see my three-year-old, Devan, holding our Siamese cat by her tail. The cat was howling and thrashing about. Before I could even think about it, I ran over to Devan, released the cat, slapped Devan's backside four or five times, and yelled, "You bad girl! Don't you ever hurt the cat like that again!"

Dan tells this tale:

It's Amy's job to do the dinner dishes. One evening she announced, "I'm too tired to do the dishes tonight—you do them." I said, "Amy, it is your job, and you will need to do it." She shouted, "I won't! And you can't make me!" I grabbed her by the arm, dragged her to her room, and yelled at her to stay there for the rest of the night.

It can be very frustrating to be a parent! Often, when the immediate goal is to just put a stop to the behavior, we get so emotionally involved in the issue that it's difficult to make a rational decision about the best course of action.

2. To Teach Children Right from Wrong

As our children mature, we hope that they will understand and accept the concept of right and wrong. We try to foster an *inner discipline* that will guide them in making the right decisions. When we punish our children, it is with the intention of teaching a lesson. We recognize that the day will eventually come when our children must go out into the world without us. We want to make sure that they go with the knowledge, skills, and abilities to make good decisions when we are not there to guide them.

3. To Make Children Understand Who Is in Charge

When our children are disrespectful, sassy, or rude, we punish with the intent of showing them who is in charge. We take control of the situation in a way that says, "*I* am the parent. *I* am in charge. You will do as I say." Sometimes this is a conscious decision based on the desire to gain control of the relationship. Sometimes, though, it is a reactionary response, based on the fact that our ego is being trampled upon! It certainly is difficult to have a two-year-old tell you, "NO!", a three-year-old yell, "I won't!", a five-year-old whine, "You can't make me!", or a ten-year-old scream, "You're not the boss over me!" It is at times like these when we want to demand the respect that is our due.

4. We Get Frustrated and Don't Know What Else to Do

We have in our mind's eye a vision—delightful, smiling children, wearing their Sunday best, and sitting side by side on the sofa. The reality is usually a very distorted image of this picture—dirty, active kids fighting over a toy that nobody really likes anyway! In our frustration to bring reality closer to our vision, we lash out and punish to try and *force* things to go our way. We really love our kids, and we really want them to behave. But sometimes they fight us so hard, and we get so frustrated, that we don't know what to do other than punish them.

> Betty and Jeff planned to take their kids, Blake and Katie, to the fair on Saturday. They anticipated a day full of quality love with their children. It didn't go that way. The kids fought all the way to the fair in the car over who was invading the other's space in the backseat. When they arrived at the fair, they fought over which direction to head first—to the amusement rides or the farm animals. They whined when Betty bought them only *one* cotton candy. Betty pleaded with them. Jeff threatened them. But the problems continued. They pestered their parents for another ride on the ponies. They said it wasn't fair when they couldn't have any ice cream. After two

hours of this, Jeff lost it. He yelled at the kids. He called them spoiled brats. He said he was sorry he ever planned this day. Betty announced that they were going home to spend the rest of the day in their rooms. Jeff said they could forget about going out for pizza that night. Blake and Katie cried all the way home, Jeff mumbled and complained, and Betty had a splitting headache.

We all want our children to behave. We want them to do so of their own free will, with no reminders, threats, or demands from us! When they don't, we often feel cornered, and we react and punish in the same ways we were punished as children. .

What Is "Punishment," and Why Doesn't It Work?

To punish, as defined by Webster's, means "to cause to undergo pain, loss, or suffering for a crime or wrongdoing." To punish implies the infliction of a penalty on a wrongdoer, and generally connotes retribution rather than correction.

Punishment puts a strain on the parent-child relationship. It doesn't teach right from wrong, doesn't put a parent in charge, and doesn't really *fix* anything. Let's look at some typical methods of punishment:

Yelling, Nagging, Threats, and Lectures

A common method of trying to control a child is with your *voice.* Witness this scene I watched in the grocery store. It is mid-afternoon at the store. A mother is shopping with her seven-year-old son.

Mother:	Mark! Come over here next to me.
Mark:	In a minute. I want to see this.
Mother:	I said *now.*
Mark:	(Walking slowly) Okay, okay. Hey! These are my favorite cookies. Can I have them?
Mother:	No. Put them back. And stop touching everything.
Mark:	Oh, come on. You never let me have what I want.
Mother:	Yes, I do. Put those down. Stop acting like this.
Mark:	(Tearing open the end of the bag) Ooops.

Mother:	Mark Allen! I told you to put those down. You're going to get it when we get home!
Mark:	(Throws the bag on the shelf, and it falls to the floor)
Mother:	You're acting like a wild animal! Stop it!

Children learn that empty threats, yelling, and nagging, while they aren't fun, rarely result in anything serious. When a parent uses his or her voice as a method of control too often, their children become "parent deaf," as we learned in Chapter 1. They use "selective hearing" to tune you out. You know what that's like: a child stares into space and says uh-huh every now and again, but then forgets everything you said. That same child, however, will come rushing down the stairs two minutes after you mention to your spouse that it would be a good night to go out for ice cream!

Spanking

Dan, a father who attended one of my classes, reported this story:

When I was three and my brother was five, my mother would spank us when we misbehaved. I used to run away to avoid the punishment. One such day, my mother reports walking by our bedroom door and hearing my brother say to me, "Don't run away when she wants to spank you. It doesn't hurt that much, and the whole thing is over. And it makes Mommy feel better, too."

Dan reports that his mother stopped spanking after that eye-opening event. Dan's brother's comments really focus on the problems with using spanking as punishment:

1. Spanking does nothing to teach a child to develop inner discipline. A child's focus is on the spanking itself, not on a review of the behavior that led to it. After a spanking, a child does not sit in his room and think, "Gee. I sure goofed. But I really learned something. Next time I'll behave." Instead a child typically is thinking, "It's not fair! She doesn't understand! I hate her!"

2. Spanking is seen as punishment for a crime, payment for a debt. In other words, once paid, they have a clean slate. Spanking gets in the way of allowing a child to develop a conscience. The guilt that follows misbehavior is a prime motivator for change. Spanking takes away the guilt, because the crime has been paid for.

3. Spanking makes the parent feel better. When we get angry, we move into the "fight or flight" mode. Our adrenaline increases, and we have a primitive need to strike out. Hitting releases this negative energy, and helps us feel better. But even a minor spanking can escalate into major abuse. Parents have reported that during the heat of the moment it's hard to stop hitting, and some say they don't even realize how hard they've hit until they see the bruise.

When you are very angry, you have several options. One, you can leave the room to cool off. Two, you can clap your hands. Clap your hands, quickly and firmly, ten or more times while stating your case: "I'm very angry at you right now. Stop this fighting!" (Try it right now, you'll see what I mean!) The neat thing about this technique is that you definitely get your child's attention, release some of your anger, and, oftentimes, it's much more effective than a smack would have been!

4. Parents who spank sometimes come to rely upon spanking as their primary source of discipline. If you give yourself permission to spank, it becomes a quick fix for all kinds of problems. It blocks off the effective use of other, more productive skills.

5. Spanking gets in the way of a healthy parent-child relationship. Children look up to their parents as protectors, teachers, and guides. When a parent breaks that pattern by hitting a child, the relationship suffers.

6. Spanking is not an effective form of discipline. Hitting a child typically stops a behavior at that point because of shock, fear, or pain. But most children turn around and repeat the same behavior—sometimes even the same day!

7. Spanking is not humane or Christian behavior. I know there are many Christian families that believe in spanking. They often quote to me from the Bible, "Spare the rod and spoil the child." Now, I am *not* an expert on the Bible, nor am I a theologian, but I am a Christian, and from that position only do I give you this opinion. I believe that the "rod" as referred to here means a tool of discipline. In the days of the Bible, a shepherd used a "rod" to guide his sheep—he did not hit them with it. His rod was seen as a symbol of his authority over the animals, not as a tool to cause them pain. I also ask you this question: if God walked into your home today and saw your child misbehave, would he hit your child? I would say definitely not! Would he discipline your child? Would he teach your child? Would he guide your child? I would say yes, absolutely!

8. Spanking does *teach a lesson. The lesson is: "When you don't know what else to do—hit!" or "When you're bigger, you can hit." or "When you're really angry, you can get your way by hitting."* It's common knowledge that children who are frequently hit are more likely to accept the use of violence, and are more likely to hit other children. It only makes sense, because, after all, children learn what they live. Children who are spanked often have more resentment and anger, and lower self-esteem.

Bribes and Rewards

If you're good, you can have a cookie. If you clean your room, I'll rent you a video. I'll give you one dollar for every A on your report card. There is a major problem with bribes and rewards—they aren't setting your children up to deal with the real world. They create false expectations in children that carry over to adulthood. When children learn to do things for the immediate reward you offer, they lose the wonderful sense of accomplishment when a job is well done—the joyful feeling of the *accomplishment* being the reward in and of itself.

> When I was in a management position, I recall having a meeting with a man named Scott whose performance was poor. During this meeting I was to issue a formal reprimand. After I explained the problems with his work, he presented his side of the story. "Look," he said, "When you guys pay me more money, I'll do a better job." I wanted to shake him and say, "Buddy, you've got it backwards! You do good work, *then* you earn more money!"

Scott's problem may have its roots in his childhood. His parents probably gave him gold stars for taking out the trash, a dollar to clean out the garage, and a big slice of cake when he ate his broccoli! Poor Scott was still looking for someone to create the motivation for him to do his best. *That's* the biggest problem with bribes and rewards. They prevent a child from developing inner motivation—those feelings that keep us working and achieving even when the payoff isn't immediate. Bribes and rewards cause a child to focus on the *reward* instead of the *activity*. This prevents a child from feeling the pure joy of accomplishment for its own sake.

Discipline—What It Is and Why It Works

Discipline, as defined by Webster's, means "training that develops self-control and character."

There are productive ways to deal with a child's misbehavior, defiance, belligerence, and other discipline problems. There are positive ways to teach right from wrong, and help a child learn the important lessons that will lead to a happier life. The main strategy involves preparing in advance for misbehavior. The more you have "pre-thought" your discipline methods, the easier it will be to deal with your children's actions. *All* children will misbehave. *Most* children misbehave in the same ways. When parents have planned their methods for dealing with the misbehavior, there are sure to be powerful, healthy results.

Use Rules and Expectations

Well-thought-out rules and routines keep parents consistent in their every-day interactions with their children. Chapter 3 gives specific details for cre-ating rules in your family. Using specific rules and routines can keep children on track, thus preventing many of the situations that may lead to misbehavior. When children know exactly what's expected of them, they are more likely to behave in ways you deem appropriate.

Parents sometimes tell me that this idea sounds like it has merit, but is a tough one to carry out. It doesn't need to be. It may take you some time to create good rules up front, but they will save you from having to deal with many small issues day after day after day. Let's review the rule-making process.

Step 1. Make a list of the repeated *misbehaviors that occur in your home.* An easy way to do this is to have a note pad handy and jot down the issues as they occur.

- Fighting
- Forgetting to do homework
- Forgetting to do chores
- Nagging, whining, sassing

Step 2. Create a simple rule for each of your top four to six issues. This is a good number to start with for several reasons. First, it's manageable. If you tried to create a rule for *every* issue that arises, you would need a *scroll*, and you would drive yourself (and your kids) crazy! Second, it forces you to focus on the big issues.

When you look at the big picture, it's often possible to cover a variety of problems with one general rule. Let's look at a sample list:

- No hurting each other
- Homework done before dinner
- Chores done before bedtime
- No sassing, whining, or nagging

Step 3. Decide on an appropriate consequence for each rule when it's broken. The consequence should be somehow connected to the misbehavior. I always marvel at the parent who, upon seeing a child hit a sibling, announces, "No TV for you tonight!" (That's kind of like being stopped for speeding by a police officer who says, "You were speeding. No skiing for you this winter!") When the consequence is related to the misbehavior, it helps teach a lesson. For example, if a child leaves his bike outside after being told to put it away, he loses the privilege of riding it the next day. In the case of the child hitting his sibling, time out makes more sense than the suspension of TV privileges.

If a child breaks her sibling's toy, she must take the money from her piggy-bank to buy (or contribute to buying) a new one.

Here are some ideas for developing appropriate consequences:

- "Call a time out"—this involves enforced "exile" of the child to a specific place for a specified amount of time. For toddlers, this might involve two minutes of sitting on the stairs or in a chair. Older children may have to go to their room, and spend a longer time by themselves. The main idea is to use separation to stop the misbehavior and cool off heated emotions (yours *and* the child's).

- Create a situation in which the child must complete a particular task before going on to things he or she would rather do.

- Take privileges away, and link them to the misbehavior, if possible.

- Restrict children to their room or the house.

- Teach the child about making amends by allowing him or her to "make it better" (buy a replacement, clean up the mess, write a note of apology).

Here are some family rules with consequences attached:

Our Family Rules

Rule	Consequence
1. No hurting each other.	Time out for five minutes, followed by apology. Must do one of your sibling's chores.
2. Homework done before dinner.	No outside play after dinner, stay in to do homework.
3. Chores done before bedtime.	Must do next morning before school (parent will wake you early).
4. No sassing, whining, or nagging.	Go to your room for ten minutes. End of the discussion on that topic.

Talk Less, Act More

Parents hinder their effectiveness by talking too much. Then they follow up all their talk with very little action. Parents who follow this pattern teach their children *not* to listen to them, and—even worse—they teach their children to ignore them, fight them, and nag them.

Watch how this parent's words get in the way of effective discipline:

Parent:	(Observing child roughly pushing his playmate at the park) Eric, don't push Nathan.
Eric:	(Continues unwanted behavior)
Parent:	Eric! Stop pushing. You need to be nice to your friend.
Eric:	(A few minutes later, he pushes Nathan again)
Parent:	Enough pushing! If you do that again, we'll have to go home.
Eric:	(A few minutes later, he pushes Nathan again)
Parent:	Okay, young man. I see you want to go home.
Eric:	No! I'm sorry. Please can we stay?
Parent:	We can't. You need to learn your lesson.
Eric:	(Starting to cry) Please, please! I'll be good.
Parent:	Oh, just stop crying. We're going.
Eric:	(Sobbing loudly) I want to stay! I'll be good. I promise! Please!!
Parent:	Okay. Just promise you won't push anymore.

With a parent like this, is it any wonder that Eric continued to push after he had been told not to? Eric has learned from experience that his mother talks but doesn't really mean what she says. All he has to do is make promises, and he can get his way. What are the chances that Eric will *really* "be good" for the remainder of his time at the park? A pattern has been set up here that puts Eric in control, and he knows it.

How could this scene be changed to demonstrate a parent who acts more and talks less?

Parent:	(Observing child roughly pushing his playmate at the park) Eric, don't push Nathan.
Eric:	(Continues unwanted behavior)
Parent:	Enough pushing! If you do that again, we'll have to go home.
Eric:	(A few minutes later, he pushes Nathan again)
Parent:	Okay, young man. I see you want to go home.

Eric:	No! I'm sorry. Please can we stay?
Parent:	No, we cannot. You have made your choice.
Eric:	(Crying, he throws himself to the ground) I don't want to go! I'll be good.
Parent:	(Picking Eric up) We're leaving now.

Listen to yourself for one day. You might be surprised at how many useless words you say. Don't try to control your children with your voice—use action. For example, instead of asking your children over and over to play nicely and share, you can quietly remove the toy and put it where they can't reach it. You don't even have to say a word for them to get the idea that they can have it back when they stop fighting over it.

Children will always test what parents say to find out if they really mean it. If parents give in repeatedly, a child learns that the parents' words are empty threats, meant to be ignored. A child will also learn by experimentation which techniques work to make you give in—crying, begging, promising, sulking, and so on. When they find the ones that work, watch out—they will use them all the time. If, on the other hand, you remain firm during these tests—when you follow through on what you say, when you refuse to be swayed—your children will abort the experiment and stop testing you. It's a very pleasant experience to say something to your children, and have them believe you rather than fight you. To some parents, it can seem like a miracle.

So give up all the empty words—give up counting to three, zip your lips, and act! You'll be amazed at the results.

Time Out

Time out can be a potent, positive disciplinary tool. It has been used effectively by parents for generations (it has its roots in that old standby, sitting in the corner). Time out works because it interrupts a child's negative behavior with space, time, and quiet. There can be three different purposes for time out. Each has its own method for successful use.

1. Stopping a specific misbehavior. Time out can be an excellent way to stop a child mid-action. It conveys a strong message that says, "This behavior is unacceptable. It will stop now." The method is especially useful with preschoolers, and is often used with great success in stopping physical violence—hitting, biting, and so on. It's effective because it allows the parent to take control of the situation immediately while still understanding that angry, out-of-control preschoolers often needs an adult's help to gain control of themselves.

Here's an example of how time out can work in this context. Danny and Alisa, brother and sister, are playing together. They begin to fight over a toy. Alisa grabs the toy, and Danny hits her.

Parent: (Taking Danny by the hand to the bathroom) Danny, no hitting. Time out.

Danny is put in the bathroom for one minute. He's then allowed to return and play with Alisa. After a while, he hits her again.

Parent: (Taking Danny by the hand to the bathroom) Danny, no hitting. Time out.

Danny is returned to the bathroom for *two* minutes. He's then allowed to return and play with Alisa. Again, he hits her.

Parent: (Taking Danny by the hand to the bathroom) Danny, no hitting. Time out.

Danny is returned to the bathroom for *three* minutes. He's then allowed to return and play with Alisa. All is peaceful.

There are several keys to using time out in this way:

1. Be quick. Catch your child in the act of misbehaving. Time out seldom works when it is delayed.

2. Use a boring place for time out, like a bathroom or a laundry room or the stairs. This is not meant to be fun. (Make sure, though, that the place is a safe one for your child to spend a few minutes alone. If no safe place is available, your child can have time out in a chair within sight of you.)

3. Use time out for selected behaviors such as hitting or backtalk. If you use time out for every misbehavior, it loses its impact.

4. Use progressive amounts of time for repeated offenses. Stick with it! When you first start using this method to stop a certain behavior, your child may spend the whole day in the bathroom! It's okay! A valuable lesson is being learned by your child ("I cannot win this one.").

5. Remember that time out used in this way stops the behavior, but does not teach a child what he should do instead. It is important that you couple time out with teaching the child about other, more peaceable options. For instance, Danny's parents need to teach him how to handle his frustration with his sister in more positive ways. One way to go about this is to watch their play carefully. Typically, when you watch a child's behavior, you can intercede before things escalate to the point of violence. Danny and Alisa are fighting over a toy. Alisa grabs the toy. You can see Danny getting mad. Now is the time to quickly intercede by walking over to Danny and talking to him. Help him by acknowledging his feelings, coach him on alternatives and model positive behavior: "Danny, I can see that you're upset about Alisa

grabbing the toy. Say to her, 'Alisa. I don't want you to grab.' Or, Danny, you can give Alisa another toy and ask her, 'Can we trade?'"

2. Giving a child the time and space to cool off and calm down. Central to using time out to cool off a child is the attitude of the parent and the explanation given the child. Of course, it won't do you much good to lecture a preschooler. But if your children are older, you can let them know your views on the subject: "Everyone needs a time out once in a while to cool off. It helps to have a place to sort out our feelings and get control of our act ions. Your angry *feelings* are okay, but your angry *actions* must be limited. If your behavior is inappropriate, I will ask you to go to your room. As soon as you feel calm and ready to behave correctly, you may come out." The purpose of using time out in this way is to teach children how to control their angry emotions. This is a valuable life skill that will prevent your children from flying off the handle, and saying—and doing—things they will later regret.

When using time out to calm an angry child, it is usually fine to send the child to his or her room. It doesn't matter whether the child holes up there and listens to the stereo, reads a book, cries, or hits a pillow. The purpose is to allow children to get control of themselves in whatever way works for them, so that they can then re-enter "society" and deal with their problem in a more productive way. Children can learn from their mistakes when adults help them understand, accept, and deal with their strong emotions. (This is an important lesson for most adults as well.)

> Rona, a professor and mother of three girls, has created an interesting variation on time out. Whenever her girls become sassy, rude, or are fighting, they are put on "Verbal Time Out"—which, as the name implies, means you must keep quiet until given permission to talk again. Rona says this is especially effective when dealing with backseat arguments in the car. She does admit to enjoying the peace and quiet in the car so much that sometimes she "forgets" to lift the ban until she hears a steady and urgent "Ummm, ummm, ummm!" from the backseat.

3. Giving a parent the time and space to cool off and calm down. There are times when we get so angry at our children that we just want to strangle them or else ground them for life! This is the time to put space between you and your child. Make a brief exit statement: "I'm so angry with you, I need a minute to think!" Then go to your room to calm down, take some deep breaths, and reflect. This will not only help you control yourself, it will provide a good role model for your child to follow.

Allowing yourself a time out when you need one can help keep your emotions under control, and remove the strain of having to deal with every situation immediately. It is also a wonderful way to model appropriate anger management for your children. (It's also a great technique for keeping a disagreement with your spouse from escalating into a full-blown argument.)

Natural Consequences

Experience is a wonderful teacher. Life has a way of teaching children things in a way that is very objective and straightforward. For example, children who don't wear their mittens will get cold hands. A child who is rude to a friend will find the friend unwilling to spend time with him. Parents would do well to let nature take over more often as their child's teacher. It can save plenty of time, and volumes of lectures, to stand back and let nature takes its course.

> It was a beautiful, snowy day. Vanessa and Angela were in the yard building a snowman when two-year-old David awoke in the morning. Barefoot and in his pajamas, he, of course, wanted to join them. I said, "Sure! Let's put on your boots and coat." Well, David would have none of that. I could tell by the way he put his hands on his hips that he was ready to do battle. This particular morning, I didn't want to fight. So I opened the door and waved him outside. David took two steps out the door, turned around, and said, "Mommy, need boots and coat!"

Do you know, I could have lectured, yelled, and threatened for *an hour*, and David would have been insistent about not wearing his boots and coat. But when I let natural consequences take over, I found that even a two-year-old can make some pretty smart decisions.

Natural consequences permit children to learn through their own actions (or *lack* of actions!). Children, in essence, become their own teachers. *Valuable learning occurs when a child is allowed to learn the hard way.* And there, in that sentence, is the *key* to the effective use of natural consequences. Read the sentence again, because the key is hidden there. The magic key is expressed in the word . . . (drum roll, please) . . . "allowed." Often parents seem determined to prevent their children from becoming frustrated or unhappy. They step in (or perhaps *rush* in) anytime their child seems ready to take a fall. This mistaken approach prevents a child from learning the many lessons that can only be learned the hard way.

It can, indeed, be difficult to stand back and watch your child suffer through a poor decision. But there are times when the best thing a parent can do is stand by and offer a shoulder and a hug.

> Anna described her nine-year-old daughter, Heather, as "bossy." She was concerned that Heather's abrupt, bossy attitude— especially with her friend Emma—would cause other kids to avoid her company. Anna said she normally "lectured" Heather after Emma's visits about how she should be more sensitive and kind to her friend, but Heather never seemed to hear her. She asked me for advice. I suggested that she just sit back and watch, and let "natural consequences" be the teacher.

A few weeks later Anna called to tell me how things were going between the two friends. She said that the last two times Heather invited Emma over to her house, Emma declined the offer. When Heather pushed her for an explanation, Emma simply said, "I just don't feel like being bossed around, okay?" Heather was crushed, and her mother was close by to comfort her.

Obviously, Heather heard her friend's words far more clearly than all her mother's previous lectures. As painful as it was for Anna to watch this, she agreed that it was important to have her daughter learn a valuable lesson about friendship.

Natural Consequences Are Enough—Keep Your Angry Emotions Out of the Picture

A very important key to letting consequences teach your child is this: use empathy and kindness to support the natural lesson. Often, parents understand the "consequence" part of this process, but miss the opportunity to help their child learn, by changing the focus of a discussion to the parent's anger. When a consequence is rolling along, a child is typically immersed in the process. But when a parent charges in full of anger, with lectures and pointing fingers, and "I told you so's," the child is pulled away from the learning process and forced to deal with the parent's anger.

Let's look at an example of a parent who starts out right—whose child is indeed in the process of learning—but then changes the focus of the situation away from the lesson onto the parent's angry feelings.

Amy, a fifth grader, has been forgetting to bring home the materials she needs for her homework assignments. Her mother is tired of reminding and nagging Amy, and driving to school to get the books and papers she needs. Because Mom has been learning about natural consequences, she decides to let the consequences of Amy's behavior teach the lesson. For an entire quarter, Mom keeps her mouth shut about homework and watches as Amy becomes more entrenched in her habit of forgetting it.

Sure enough, when Amy brings her report card home, her grades have dropped, and the teacher has added a note saying, "Amy's low grades this period reflect her neglect of her homework. She has the skills and ability to achieve much higher grades."

Mom takes a look at the report card and says, "Amy. This is so sad. It must really hurt to get grades like this when you know you're capable of much better work. I bet you wish you would have done a better job on your homework. Gee, if you keep this up, you'll be taking fifth grade over again next year while Sara and Betsy go on to sixth grade without you." Amy starts to cry. (A good sign—it indicates ownership of the problem and regret for the mistake.)

So far, Mom has done a perfect job of letting consequences be the teacher. She can stop now, and perhaps cue her husband to repeat the process when he sees the report card; and offer her assistance in getting her daughter more organized. But watch how her old habits creep in and spoil the effect of the lesson for Amy, and change the direction of Amy's thoughts. Mom just can't help herself. She dives in headfirst with her old habits:

"Since homework seems to be the problem, you can stay home every weekday after school until you can bring up these grades and prove to be responsible. And you can forget about having Sara and Betsy over Friday night for a sleep-over! I expect you to think about this report card for a while. This really makes me mad!"

Amy's tears suddenly turn to anger, "That's not fair! You're so mean! It's not my fault I forget my homework. Mr. Jones doesn't remind me, and you always forget to remind me, too. And he gives us too much homework, anyway. And you didn't get me any of the markers I need for my homework! It's not my fault! It's no fair!"

Amy stomps off to her room to—think about her bad grades? No way. She thinks about how mean her mother is, and how unfair Mr. Jones is.

It would have been far more productive for Mom to have let Amy feel the consequences of her behavior, and to have sat down with her for a problem-solving session. She could have helped Amy create a schedule for homework, as well as helping her develop a method for remembering to bring it home. This would have been much more effective than grounding her and canceling her sleep-over.

Parents should try to keep their own emotions out of such situations. By getting angry, we rob our children of the *privilege* of feeling their pain over the consequences of their behavior. We can instead guide, direct, and assist. These actions, along with empathy ("Too bad," "That must hurt," "If that happened to me, I'd sure be embarrassed," "Oh dear," "I bet this makes you sad"...) are the best complement to natural consequences.

When you use consequences to allow your children to learn valuable lessons, you are one step closer to meeting your major goal as a parent. No, the goal is not to control kids and make them behave. The major goal is to help your kids grow to be happy, secure, self-motivated, and successful adults who can think for themselves.

Logical Consequences

There are times when we *cannot* allow a natural consequence to occur, because it would be too severe or too expensive. You can't let your child get hit by a car to teach crosswalk safety. And you don't want your child's new bike stolen to teach responsibility. And then there are times when there is no natural consequence that will occur on its own.

At times like these you can make use, instead, of logical consequences. Logical consequences are those that you arrange or enforce as a result of your child's actions or lack of actions. Logical consequences are most effective when a child can clearly see the connection between the behavior and the consequence. Here are two examples:

> Leslie told me of the problem with her eight-year-old, Shannon, who dawdles each morning, and makes all three kids late for school. Leslie explained, "After learning about logical consequences, I formed a plan. I woke Shannon and reminded her that we would leave the house at 8:00 sharp for school. Then I kept quiet and went about my own business. When Shannon finally came downstairs, the other two kids were in the car ready to take off with Dad for school. Shannon announced that she had yet to brush her hair, brush her teeth, or eat breakfast. I said that her hair and teeth would go unbrushed, and ushered a very tearful Shannon out the door with a baggie of dry cereal. The next morning, she was the *first* kid down to the kitchen for breakfast! It's been two whole weeks, and she's been on time every day. This was so much more effective than all my previous yelling and pleading!"

> Michelle and Loren used logical consequences effectively with their ten-year-old daughter, Sarah. It seems that Sarah was using two or three towels after each bath, and filling the hamper with them. Loren had explained that a towel could be re-used several times before washing, but his message wasn't sinking in. Loren and Michelle decided to let logical consequences become the teacher. Sarah was notified that she had a new chore: laundering the towels. Loren reports that the family now has a "towelhawk" who carefully monitors *everyone's* towel usage!

Logical consequences are by far most effective when they directly relate to the misbehavior. A child *cannot* understand why he must go a week without TV because he left his new bike at the park. He *can* understand losing his privilege of riding his bicycle for a week after leaving it at the park.

An important point regarding the use of logical consequences: a parent can rarely come up with the right consequence on the spot, particularly when upset. It's better to let your child know how unhappy you are, explain that you don't yet know how you're going to handle the situation, and take your time to decide on an appropriate consequence. This delay tactic is in itself a very powerful tool to use in teaching your children how to feel responsibility for their misbehavior, because while you are deciding, your child will be worrying. Watch how this works:

> Amy had a habit of borrowing her mother's sweatshirts without asking. She had been told numerous times to get permission first. On one occasion, Amy returned Mom's shirt without having told her she'd borrowed it. Her mother later found the sweatshirt in her closet, spotted with dark paint. Mom brought the shirt into Amy's room and said, "I'm very angry about this. I don't know what I'm going to do about it, but I'll let you know." Later that day, Amy asked, "Have you decided about the shirt yet?" Mom replied, "No, but I'll let you know when I do." The next day Amy called her mother twice at work to inquire about the impending decision. Amy was obviously doing quite a bit of thinking about the shirt! That evening, Amy came up to her mother and said, "I'm real sorry about your shirt. I called the store, and it costs $23. Here's the money. Next time I'll get permission."

Children don't always come up with their own solutions. Nevertheless, when they have time to think about their infraction, this often creates a sense of ownership of the problem in their own mind. As a result, when the parent announces the consequence, it is often accepted without argument. (I think this is because the consequence is rarely as bad as all the doom-and-gloom that the child has been coming up with using his or her active imagination!)

Distraction and Avoidance

All parents have days when they feel like they're about to "lose it" with their kids. Sometimes, it's because you are just having a bad day. Sometimes, it's because your kids are doing everything to push your buttons: begging for a cookie *again*, fighting and arguing *again*, whining and fussing *again*, neglecting their pet *again!* You know that feeling when you just wish you could pack a suitcase and take a vacation! Well, here's an approach that can give you lots of little "vacations" from parenting.

The approach I call "distraction and avoidance" gives you the privilege of taking off your teacher's hat once in a while. It gives you permission to let a few little issues slide. It says that it's okay to *choose* to be inconsistent once in a while.

How can you best use distraction and avoidance? First, make a conscious decision to use this skill, and to feel okay about using it right now. (In other words, don't use it "by accident" and deceive yourself: *"Oh, I didn't just see Josh hit Jessica . . . again. I think he just bumped up against her."*) Instead *decide* to ignore a given behavior by using these steps:

Step 1. Take a deep breath and relax. Realize that this *one issue* will not make or break your child's entire future. Sometimes, peace and quiet can be more important than *any one particular argument.* Give yourself permission to step away from your teacher's podium this one time.

Step 2. Divert their attention. Snap your fingers, or clap your hands, and say, "Hey!" Then distract your kids and yourself from the situation at hand.

"Hey! Is that a cat at the window?"

"Hey! Who wants to order pizza?"

"Hey! I just remembered the words to that song. Listen."

Step 3. Forget about the problem. Move on with life! There will be many more times when a lesson can be taught. For now—enjoy a mini-vacation from parenting.

You have just changed everyone's focus and avoided an argument. I call this a parent's "secret weapon" for keeping peace and harmony in the home. This enables you to pick your battles based not only on importance, but also on your current frame of mind.

I have found that this skill is a lifesaver when you have more than one child under the age of five—especially if one of them is a baby! I have heard so many, many parents descend on their firstborn when the second baby arrives with an abundance of *Nos, Don'ts, and Stops.* (I firmly believe those to be the words that fertilize sibling rivalry!) Instead, become a master at distraction and avoidance. Couple this with good modeling, gentle teaching, lots of praise when praise is due, and loving attention—and you have a recipe for peace of mind and the encouragment of positive behavior.

Obviously, this method is not meant to be overused. And it should never be used when some truly horrifying situation is at hand, such as violence or sexual abuse. However, when used in combination with all the other skills and techniques available to you, distraction and avoidance can be a very powerful addition to your repertoire of coping strategies.

Behavior Baseball

One of the major frustrations of parenthood is when you have to deal with the same problem over and over and over and over again. Whether it's the dog that never gets fed, or the bicycle that never makes it to the garage, or the homework that never gets done—it's *so* frustrating to feel ineffective with your children!

When my daughter Angela turned six, we finally gave in to her desire for a pet and bought her a guinea pig. Ginger was the center of Angela's world—for about two months. Then, Angela's other priorities got in the way of making sure that her pet had food, water, and a clean cage. I tried all my skills:

I made a clear statement of fact: "Ginger needs food and water and a clean cage every day to be happy and healthy." I tried Grandma's Rule: "After you feed Ginger, you may have your breakfast." I gave clear instructions, and used a regular routine: "Ginger needs to have food and water every day before breakfast, and her cage needs to be cleaned every Tuesday and Saturday." I made it brief: "Ginger's hungry." I gave Angela a choice: "Do you want to take care of Ginger now or after lunch?" I made something talk: "Angela, it's me, Ginger! My cage is so smelly—pee-euw! Please give me some clean litter!" I wrote Angela a note, and used humor: "Ginger is cute and Ginger is sweet, but her dirty cage smells like rotten feet."

After my virtuoso performance of all my sophisticated parenting skills, Ginger was still my problem and not Angela's. I finally got *very* tired of the daily battle. I wasn't the one who wanted a guinea pig. I wanted Angela to be responsible for her own pet. I wanted to set the stage for all the future dogs, cats, birds, and fish that would grace our family in the years to come. I sat down, pen in hand, and thought about this issue. Finally I came up with the perfect solution.

The idea came to me while watching Angela play T-ball that Saturday. *Three strikes and you're out!* I decided that we were going to play *behavior baseball*. I created this sign:

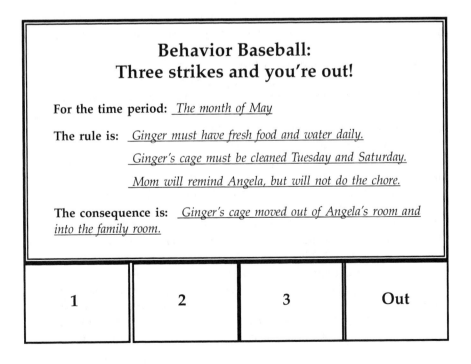

Behavior Baseball:
Three strikes and you're out!

For the time period: *The month of May*

The rule is: *Ginger must have fresh food and water daily.*

Ginger's cage must be cleaned Tuesday and Saturday.

Mom will remind Angela, but will not do the chore.

The consequence is: *Ginger's cage moved out of Angela's room and into the family room.*

| 1 | 2 | 3 | Out |

The consequence for the month of June was: **Ginger's cage moved to the basement rec-room.**

The consequence for the month of July was: **Sell Ginger.**

I gave a lot of thought to the consequences. I tried to make sure that they were directly related to Ginger. (I would not, for instance, take away Angela's rollerblades.) It was very important to Angela to have Ginger in her room: moving Ginger downstairs would be very painful. Since Angela rarely went to the rec-room, moving Ginger there was the equivalent, in Angela's mind, to moving Ginger to Siberia. And selling Ginger was, of course, the last-resort solution to the problem. I thought this through very carefully in advance, and decided that, yes, I was willing to live with the pain of selling Angela's pet—and Angela's guilt—if it would teach *all of my children* a very important lesson: *if it's your pet, you are expected to take care of it. If Mom wants a pet of her own, she will get a pet of her own.*

I chose a quiet time to sit down with Angela and review the new plan. Needless to say, she was not very happy with me. She began to cry and plead with me to keep Ginger. I explained that the power to keep Ginger was hers alone. If she followed the schedule, everything would be just fine.

At first, of course, it was *not* just fine. A few days later, when Angela was having breakfast, I mentioned that Ginger's water bottle was empty. Angela said, "I'll fill it later." After Angela had left for school, Ginger began banging her water bottle—because it was, of course, still empty. I filled it. I used a black permanent marker, and I put an X on the chart for "strike one." When Angela came home from school and saw her first X, she became hysterical. "You don't understand! I was going to do it when I came home! I didn't understand! It's not fair!" She then ripped the chart off the refrigerator, wadded it up, and threw it in the trash! I calmly retrieved the chart, smoothed out the wrinkles, and taped it back on the refrigerator.

A few calm days passed. It was again morning and I mentioned to Angela that Ginger's bowl was empty. I even offered a choice: "Would you like to do it now, or after you finish dressing?" Time passed, and Angela again went off to school forgetting her pet. I filled the bowl and marked another X on strike two. Angela returned from school that day and . . . ditto the above story . . . (except she didn't rip off the chart, because she figured I would just put it back up again). Now, however, Angela finally understood the reality of the consequences. She asked me for a piece of poster board, and sat down at the table with her marking pens. Of her own free will, she created a "reminder calendar" for her pet-care responsibilities, and hung it on her bedroom door. The calendar had a box for each day, which Angela could X out after she was done—the chart had 236 boxes!

Angela did get a few more strikes, but they were few and far between. What was most important was that she developed her own routine for fulfilling her pet-care chores. Soon the chart became unnecessary, and we took it down. That doesn't mean that it will stay down forever. Kids (and grown-ups, too) have a way of slipping back into old bad habits. When and if Ginger becomes an issue again, we will re-establish the Behavior Baseball chart in our household.

A few pointers to keep in mind when using Behavior Baseball:

- Use this technique for major repeat problems and use it for only one issue at a time. If you cover your refrigerator with baseball charts, your child could become a nervous wreck and fail at everything! Examples of appropriate issues, in addition to pet-care routines, might include problems relating to homework, chores, sibling aggression, curfews, and bedtime routines.

- Use realistic time periods, rules, and consequences. Don't make things so difficult that your child has no chance of success. Make sure you take your child's age, personality, and current lifestyle into consideration.

- Don't bargain over strikes. If the rule was broken, a strike has been earned. (That's why it's important to think through your consequences very cautiously beforehand, making sure that you're completely willing to follow through on them if necessary.)

- It's still okay to give a reminder when called for. After all, you *do* want your child to succeed.

Problem-Solving Together

Earlier we talked about asking children helpful questions as a method of encouraging them to think for themselves and explore their own ideas. Problem solving is just an expansion of that idea: you involve them in helping to look for solutions to a given problem. Problem solving is effective because children are given the respect and encouragement to become involved in taking care of themselves. These are the basic steps involved in problem solving:

1. Choose a quiet, uninterrupted time to address a problem.

2. Start by defining the problem in unemotional terms.

3. Let your child give his or her side of the story. Listen quietly.

4. Discuss as many possible solutions as you can come up with together.

5. Jointly decide which solution you will use, and follow through.

The key to having a successful problem-solving session is to remember that you are *working together* with your child to arrive at a solution. If you have one solution in mind, and nothing else will satisfy you, then this isn't the right technique to use at the moment. Problem solving will only work if you are willing to be flexible and open to your child's ideas.

I have seen parents use this technique successfully to solve problems relating to homework, sibling issues, chores, bedtime battles, curfews, pet care, sports or music lessons, allowance, and other ongoing issues. The beauty of the method is that typically, when children are involved in the problem-solving process, they are far more likely to follow through with the solution than if you had forced your own solution upon them.

Many people ask at what age a child is old enough to help problem-solve. I *used* to think that a child needed to be of school age to use this method, until my two-and-a-half-year-old son taught me otherwise.

> David had been potty trained for some time, but we had a continuing problem with his waiting until the last possible minute and dribbling in his pants each time. Changing his pants eight times a day was getting to be a real pain. I was wondering how to handle this when one day we just sort of stumbled into a problem-solving session. I was explaining the problem to David, and asked a rhetorical question, "How can we solve this?" He actually answered me. "I know," he said. "When Daddy's home, I won't dribble." "Oh?" I looked at him blankly (trying very hard not to laugh). "And," he continued, "When Daddy's at work, I won't dribble." "Well, that sounds like a good idea," I said. And as he walked away I was scratching my head, wondering just where that came from! Later that day, David ran past me to the bathroom saying, "Daddy's at work, so I better not dribble!" Believe it or not, his solution worked.

Now, keep in mind, David's solution worked precisely because it was *his solution*. If I had said to him, "Now David, I don't want you dribbling in your pants when Daddy's at work. And I don't want you dribbling when Daddy's at home. Understand?", he probably would have stared at me blankly and gone on dribbling all day long. But because it was *his* idea—however absurd—it made an impression on him, and he was able to follow through with it. It also filled him with a sense of pride at discovering the solution on his own.

Patience, Practice, and Persistence

You now have many new skills for encouraging your child's cooperation, providing the foundation for realistic and effective discipline. Remember to use these ideas as guidelines for creating the methods that work best for you and your family. Try out each idea for a long enough period of time to give it a realistic chance for success. You may feel awkward or strange when trying these techniques, especially if they're very different from what you've done before. Bear in mind that exercising these techniques won't merely change your child—they'll change you as well. Parents often tell me that, over time, their new skills become so much a part of their lives that it's hard to remember what things were like before. Implementing these changes does take patience, though, and lots of practice. You cannot just read through this book once and expect to be miraculously transformed into a "perfect parent." I strongly suggest that you post the Reminder Pages (the last page from each of Chapters 2–8) on your refrigerator, or in other highly visible places, to help you remember the skills you're learning. I find that focusing on one reminder page at a time, for about a month, is usually best. If you post all of them, they tend to become wallpaper: you see them, but you don't pay them any mind.

Most importantly, be patient with yourself! The more you know, the more critical you can become of your parenting methods. Parents often tell me stories of their mistakes, expressing embarrassment and guilt over "doing it wrong." Actually, this kind of acknowledgment is the first major step in making a change. When you can tell that you are "doing it wrong," and can clearly identify what you should have done instead, then you really are starting to understand the philosophy behind this book. Mastery will just take practice and persistence: soon you will be doing such a good job overall that you will be able to forgive yourself your mistakes. Remember, we all make mistakes—that's part of being human. It's really okay! Your kids will benefit greatly if you use your skills and knowledge even 50 percent of the time.

So, give yourself a break, do your best, and move forward.

Reminder Page—Punishment Versus Discipline

Use Rules and Expectations

Write them down; include consequences.

Talk Less, Act More

Think first. When you say it, mean it.

Time Out

Provide space to cool off and calm down. Be quick.

Natural Consequences

Let your child learn through experience. Support the lesson with empathy.

Logical Consequences

Consequences should always be related to the problem, and dispensed without anger.

Distraction and Avoidance

Choose your battles. Take a mini-vacation.

Behavior Baseball

Use this technique for repeat problems. Rules are written down and specific. Three strikes and you're out.

Problem-Solve Together

Involve your child in finding a solution.

Practice, Patience, Persistence

Be kind to yourself. Allow time for changes to occur.

5

Building Your Child's Self-Esteem

Monica is slowly drifting awake. She feels her mother's gentle caress, and hears her sweet voice saying, "Good morning, Princess—time to rise and shine!" Monica stretches and pulls herself out of bed. She dresses, and then wanders into the bathroom. As she is brushing her hair, she accidentally knocks over a bottle of shampoo and it spills all over. "Oh, darn," she says, as she grabs a towel and mops it up. Just then her mother walks by and says, "Ooops, I see you've had an accident. Thanks for cleaning it up. It's 7:30—breakfast is on the table." Monica has breakfast and packs her lunch. She comments to her mother that she has a big test in math today, and she's nervous. Her mom kisses the top of her head and says, "You did a lot of studying. I have confidence that you'll do well." Monica grabs her lunch and heads out the door for school. Her mom calls from the kitchen, "Monica! Your homework is on the table!" Monica rushes in, grabs her papers, says, "Thanks, Mom!" and heads out the door as she hears her mom say, "I love you, Princess—have a great day."

On the school bus, Monica's friend sits with another girl and giggles, and they both look over at Monica. She tries to ignore them, and sits down next to her friend Sally, and begins chatting. When Monica steps off the bus, she knows why they were giggling—she has on one purple sneaker and one blue one! She points to her feet and says laughingly to Sally, "Look! I bet I start a new style—everyone's gonna want to wear two different shoes now!" Sally laughs, and they head off to their classroom.

Meanwhile, a few blocks away, Lynn is slowly drifting awake. She hears her mother's voice blasting, "Lynn! Will you get out of bed already! Why do I always have to call you five times! You're going to be late." Lynn stretches and pulls herself out of bed. She dresses, and then wanders into the bathroom. As she is brushing her hair, she accidentally knocks over a bottle of shampoo and it spills all over. "Oh, I'm such a klutz," she says, as she grabs a towel and mops it up. Just then her mother walks by and says, "Lynn, you are such a klutz! And why are you using the good towel to clean that up! Oh, you're not getting it all, here, let me do it. It's past 7:30, and breakfast is on the table. Get down there and eat, or you'll be late again." Lynn has breakfast and complains about the sandwich her mother is packing in her lunch. Her mother says, "That's all I ever hear are complaints. You'll eat it or go hungry."

Lynn comments to her mother that she has a big test in math today, and she's nervous. Her mom says, "If you had studied last night, like I told you to, you wouldn't be worried now." Lynn grabs her lunch and heads out the door for school. Her mom calls from the kitchen, "Lynn! Your homework is on the table! I swear, if your head wasn't connected, you'd leave it behind, too." Lynn rushes in, grabs her papers, says, "Bye, Mom!" and heads out the door. On the school bus, Lynn's friend sits with another girl and giggles, and they both look over at Lynn. She sits down in another seat and pretends to read a book, but she's really wondering, "Why are they laughing at me? I bet they don't like me anymore." When Lynn steps off the bus, she knows why they were giggling—she has on one purple sneaker and one blue one. Tears fill her eyes as she starts to plan a stomachache so she can go to the nurse's office and maybe even be sent home for the day.

There is a definite relationship between the way you raise your children and the level of happiness and success they will achieve in life. Positive, effective parenting has the greatest chance of reaping the reward of successful, happy children who grow into successful, happy adults. What is the greatest gift you can give your children? Healthy self-esteem: that sense of inner happiness that doesn't depend on input from the outside; the ability to see themselves as inherently valuable and worthwhile; the ability to experience life with the flexibility, receptivity, and honesty that can make every day satisfying. You cannot control your child's life or future. You cannot determine your child's profession, marital choices, parenting choices, or where and how they choose to live. You can and will, however, have a dramatic effect on your child's self-esteem. This is not something that happens overnight. It is not contingent upon any *one* thing. Rather, it is based on your *attitude* and the many subtle interactions that occur between you and your children every day. Dr. Larry Koenig, creator of the national Up With Youth program, has said, "Self-esteem is molded mainly by parents, whether they plan it or not!"

In this chapter we will talk about very specific ways you can build your children's self-esteem. We will take a closer look at how our words and actions affect our children's view of themselves, and the ways in which we can make these views positive.

Choose Your Words Carefully

Our children create their images of themselves mostly through the input they receive from us, particularly during their early years. Children look to us to validate their existence as distinct individuals. They're extremely sensitive to all the cues we give them—both verbal and nonverbal—about who they are. Children instinctively long for their parents' love and approval. A child who is acting out is sending a desperate message about some basic need that's going unmet, whether a need for structure, limits, attention, time, or more affection. Because they're children, they can't articulate these needs. And because we're human, we won't always be able to second-guess them. All we can do as parents is do our best to convey through words, gestures, and deeds that our children are important, worthwhile, and distinct human beings who will grow stronger and more self-sufficient as time goes on (and let them know without a doubt that we will always, even in times of conflict, love them).

The many daily interchanges we have with our children are like the individual building blocks that go into making a large building. Each block is important in creating the structure, just as each day's events are important in the formation of our children's self-concept.

Here's a sampler of destructive comments parents may unknowingly make to their children:

"Bad boy [girl]!"

"You never listen!"

"Don't be so stupid!"

"Look at you—who'd want to be friends with you, anyway?"

"What is the matter with you?"

"You'd forget your head if it wasn't attached."

"Look at this clean bedroom! What a shock! I can't believe it! I must be in the wrong house."

"*You're* . . . such a slob . . . so clumsy . . . so nasty . . . so rude . . . so lazy . . . so careless . . . such a brat."

"Why do you *always* do that?"

"Is this the best you could do?"

"You just didn't try hard enough."

"I worked twice as hard when I was your age."

"Can't you two get along for one minute?"

"Grow up!"

"You never listen to me."

"Don't be a crybaby!"

"There's no reason to be so upset!"

"You're a lost cause—I give up!"

"You can't imagine how ugly you look with that haircut!"

Take a close look at these statements. Can you see how hurtful they are to the fragile self-esteem of a child or adolescent? Even a comment disguised as a compliment or joke will be taken at face value. The underlying message is "You're worthless and inadequate. And, not only that, but that's all I expect of you."

It's important that you listen to yourself when you talk to your children, especially during those times when you're unhappy with their behavior. Even the child who seems to be tuning you out completely is taking in every word of implied or direct criticism you utter. That's why it's essential when you criticize to make sure you direct your words at your child's behavior, not at his identity or personality.

How can you talk to your children to build their self-esteem and help them create a positive picture of themselves? First, *think* about what you say. It takes more effort to choose your words carefully than it does to use clichés, or just say the first thing that comes to your mind. Try to phrase your comments *positively*. Point out what you *want to see* rather than what you *don't want to see*. Here are some examples:

Negative	Positive
Don't forget your lunch!	Remember your lunch!
How many times do I have to tell you?	I should only have to tell you once.
Don't be so rude!	I know you have good manners, and I expect you to use them.
You got 100 percent! I can't believe it!	Wow, 100 percent. You must be so proud!

Why do you kids have to be so noisy?	Please play more quietly.
You never listen to me!	I expect you to listen to me.
You always make such a mess.	Please clean up your art supplies as soon as you are done working.
Where are your manners? Were you born in a barn?	What I expect you to say is, "No thank you, I don't care for any."

Jimmy Johnson, the renowned former coach of the Dallas Cowboys, used this technique with his players. He was known for saying, "Protect the ball" (instead of "Don't fumble") or "Make this one" (instead of "Don't miss it"). His post-game meetings focused his players' thoughts forward to "how we can win the next game," instead of rehashing a loss. Under Johnson's positive leadership, the Cowboys won the Super Bowl in 1993 and 1994.

Your children look up to you. They believe in you, and they trust you. Your words carry more importance to them than anyone else's words. Use this power in a positive, encouraging way!

Help Your Children Develop Positive Thinking Skills

During their growth and development, children go through many stages of self-doubt and fear. They are always comparing themselves to others, and they often see themselves as coming up short. As parents, we can offset this natural tendency in our children by giving them the skills to think more positively. It is important that you really listen to your children, and help them overcome their negative thoughts. This is, of course, easier to do if *you* practice positive thinking yourself (see Chapter 8).

Our world is so full of negative feedback. We need to arm our children with a positive attitude, so that they can stay focused in the right direction. Let's look at some typical negative statements from children, along with some positive responses from their parents:

Child's Negative Statement	**Parent's Positive Response**
I can't do it.	Take your time and try again. I have confidence in you.
Heather hates me.	Sounds like you're feeling rejected by Heather. That must hurt. I know you want Heather to like you. Try to remember that you're a very lovable kid, and a terrific person, no matter what Heather says or does

	right now. You know, she may be having some problem that has nothing to do with you.
I'm just no good in history.	You've brought up Cs before—I know you can do it again. And look at this A in math!
I'm so clumsy. I'll never learn to rollerblade!	It's tough learning something new. Remember when you first tried skates, how hard it was? But you stuck with it, and now you're really good at skating.

There is real value in *discussing* positive thinking and self-esteem with your children on a regular basis. Sadly, these subjects are not yet included in the school curriculum. There are good books written for children of all ages, as well as adults, which demonstrate the use of positive thinking. Reading a book together is a good launching pad for starting a conversation. Pointing out positive versus negative attitudes from news stories or life stories is an excellent way of showing your children just how this all works in real life, too. Modeling a positive attitude is one of the *most effective* ways of teaching your children. Children learn what they live.

Parents always *hope* that their children will have a positive outlook on life, but most often how this happens is left to chance. When you take this matter into your hands, and look for ways to guide your children's thoughts in a positive direction, you will see very exciting results.

Develop Your Children's Best Qualities

All children have talents, abilities, and areas of strength. They may excel in academics, music, art, sports, or communication; they may have a natural talent for humor, a tremendously gentle or generous nature, or an infectious energy and enthusiasm for life. The point is that every individual human being has something special to offer the world, and a unique set of reasons for being valued. Parents play a significant role in determining if a child grows up with a strong sense of his or her own special gifts, and a joy in exercising them. Without acknowledgment and nurturing, skills and talents have a way of fading, stagnating, or being hidden away.

A parent's loving guidance can strengthen and expand a child's innate abilities. Children who are nurtured and accepted in this way are far more likely to feel capable, talented, and in control of their destiny. Such feelings greatly enhance a child's (and the subsequent adult's) self-esteem. A feeling of expertise in one area will positively affect all areas of a child's life.

You can help develop your child's strengths in a number of ways. First, give your child opportunities to try out many new experiences. If you pay attention, you'll get lots of information about what new experiences will complement your child's process of figuring out exactly who he or she is. Does your child love music? Dance? Does there seem to be a deficit in self-confidence or self-discipline that might disappear with involvement in one of the martial arts? Would your preschooler's bubbling energy find a good outlet in a gymnastics class?

There are almost endless possibilities for extracurricular classes, but these aren't the *only* possibilities. For a young child, many of *your* chores can turn into exciting learning experiences if the child is allowed to participate, and is given some responsibility. Grocery shopping can turn from a dreaded experience into one that's pleasurable for both of you if you find meaningful ways for your toddler to participate. Go to the appropriate aisles and have your child "find" a familiar item for you and put it in the cart. Let him or her transfer the lighter items from the cart to the check-out counter. Have the clerk pack a special (lightweight) sack for your child to carry out of the store. When parents foster this kind of responsible behavior in their children, the payoffs are great, both in terms of public behavior and the child's sense of self-worth and mastery.

When children try something new, and seem to like it or do well at it, give them the positive encouragement to keep practicing. Try to stress the inherent joy in mastery, rather than suggesting that mastery will make your child more lovable. In other words, make sure your child knows that your love is based on identity rather than accomplishments. Make it a habit to point out your children's strengths to them. Often, we get so busy with life that we pass up many opportunities to build up our children through compliments: "Wow! What a high tower! You sure know how to build!" "That was a pretty tune—did you make that up?" "Look at how quickly you got through all those math problems!" Carry on with this appreciation right on through your child's adolescence and into adulthood. "You have an amazing sense of style—I never would have thought of putting that dress together with those boots." Individuals who feel loved and appreciated by their parents have a leg up on life. They will be much more likely to feel an inner sense of worth, uniqueness, and value, and will be able to fall back on this love at those difficult times when things go wrong.

Praise and Encourage

You are driving home from work. The radio is on, and you're singing along, looking forward to getting home and putting your feet up. You glance in your rearview mirror and see a police car behind you—and his lights are on! As you pull over, your heart begins to pound, and your hands begin to sweat. You think, "Oh, no. What did I do?" The officer saunters up to your window and asks for your license and registration. You dump the contents of your wallet on the seat beside you, and finally come up with the right documents. The officer glances at your license, removes his glasses, looks you in the eye, and says, "I just wanted to say, 'Thanks.' I've been driving behind you, and you are a courteous, exemplary driver. I would like to give you this Safe Driver Certificate and my compliments. Have a nice day!"

After the shock wore off, how do you suppose you would feel? Proud? Happy? Important? How many people would you tell this story to? As you drive on down the road, what are the chances you will let the person in front of you merge as you smile and wave them on? How long would the glow last? When a person of authority (a police officer, a parent) gives sincere praise, the recipient (you, your child) feels acknowledged and pleased. Praise also encourages you to repeat the behavior, and its effects are carried over to other parts of your life as well.

Praise, encouragement, and appreciation are the desserts of life. We look forward to them, savor them, and can never have enough of them! They boost our self-esteem, and encourage us to do even better in life. The effects are lasting and cumulative. A beautiful side effect is that we feel good about the person doing the praising.

In terms of motivating change, praise is also a very powerful tool. It's more effective than either material rewards or punishment in encouraging positive behaviors in our children. Praise encourages your children to make improvements on their own.

Don't ever think you can give too much praise to your child. Sincere praise, approval, and appreciation are among the best gifts you can bestow.

Listen with Your Heart

It's tough growing up. Think back to when *you* were growing up, and all the times when you felt self-doubt, confusion, and frustration. You can help your children get through the bumps and bruises of childhood by simply *being there for them*. Children need to know that when the whole world feels like it's crashing down around them, they have one safe, secure place to go, and one bottomless source of unconditional love.

Listening is as much a skill as giving a speech. It's not just a matter of picking up sounds: *active listening* involves an array of behaviors that express your attention, empathy, and respect. Listening to your children in this way will go far toward convincing them of your unconditional love. Keep these guidelines in mind when your child has something important to say to you:

1. Put down your paper or dish towel. Shut off the TV. Maintain as much eye contact as your child seems comfortable with. Make body contact if that seems appropriate. Often, when children are trying to express a problem, thought, or concern, their parents say they're listening, but half of their attention is somewhere else. You can't con a

child in this way. Typically, a few minutes of sincere, attentive listening is worth more than an hour of letting your child talk while you carry on with another activity.

2. Don't rush to jump in with solutions, ideas, or lectures. Often, children just need a sounding board. They need another person listening to give them an opportunity to figure out exactly what they want to do. Solving your child's problem may give you the relief of ending his or her discomfort; but, in the long term, it's worth far more to children to get the support they need to formulate solutions on their own. Jumping in with a judgmental comment such as "I told you so!" will only make your child far less likely to consult with you next time a problem comes up.

3. Demonstrate that you're listening by asking appropriate questions and making "listening" sounds: "Hmm," "Gee!" "Really?" "Darn!" (Of course, you'll want to gear these to your own speech patterns and vocabulary, as well as to your child's age.)

4. Validate your child's fears, feelings, and worries. When our children come to us with negative emotions, it's far too tempting to minimize them: "Oh, don't worry about it!" "There's nothing to be afraid of." Such comments do much more harm than good. It's very important for children as part of their development to learn to trust their own feelings, and to listen to them. By brushing them off, you're giving your child the message that his or her feelings are inaccurate, wrong, or unimportant. Such children grow up to be adults who either suppress their feelings, or are so out of touch with them that they don't even know what they are, much less possess the language to talk about them. You can validate your child's feelings instead with such comments as, "That sure sounds embarrassing." "It can hurt so much to feel left out," or "I know you're feeling scared now."

5. Help your child focus on possible solutions, rather than getting mired in the problem. If the situation isn't one that can be solved—if it's a condition rather than a problem—encourage your child to express his or her feelings fully, and then move on. ("Children can be very cruel sometimes. We can't control the way other people behave. The most we can do is to be kind ourselves, and hope that the goodness spreads itself around. And goodness has a way of doing that.") Help move your child towards more positive thinking. Use forward-thinking phrases like, "I bet you wish . . ." or "Wouldn't it be nice if . . ." or "What do you think you'll do now?" or "Would you like to hear my ideas about that?"

Years ago, I remember reading about a man who had five grown sons—all happy, successful adults with high and healthy self-esteem. The man was asked what he felt he did to encourage his sons' success. Without hesitation, he explained that all the while they were growing up, they had an after-dinner ritual they would follow. Each boy was given a certain day of the week, and on his day, when the other boys were cleaning up after dinner, the man would take that son out to the porch and they would sit on the swing together. He said he always let the boy set the pace for their time together. Sometimes they would have a serious talk, sometimes light conversation, and sometimes they would just sit in companionable silence. These boys could count on their dad to listen to them, to be there for them, to care. Their father's gift of listening was a powerful influence on the lives of these five young men.

Love Is the Wind Beneath Our Wings

For children, the most powerful builder of healthy self-esteem is the knowledge that they are loved. Totally. Uniquely. Unconditionally. Without this love, it is difficult if not impossible for children to feel a secure inner sense of their importance and value. If your children know that their place in your world is secure, they will have the confidence to move out into the bigger, wider world.

I know you love your child, or you wouldn't be reading this book. But you cannot simply assume that your child feels secure in your love. You must show your love to your child on a daily basis. All people—children as well as adults—need to feel love in many ways to feel convinced of its presence. Here are some of the ways in which you can show your children love:

Use good parenting skills. Children whose parents yell, nag, lecture, and threaten will constantly question their parents' love for them. Children whose parents use positive skills on a regular basis will feel loved because of the secure, solid discipline, and the supportive environment, in which they grow.

Accept your child for who he or she is. A child feels loved when you appreciate and understand that child's unique personality and identity. When a child chronically feels criticized, or feels that a parent is always trying to transform the child into someone different, he or she will not feel loved. Even if some of your child's basic characteristics are painful to you—if you wish that your shy child were more outgoing, or your aggressive child were gentler—it's important to realize that your child hasn't *chosen* to be aggressive or shy. Most such basic characteristics are biologically determined. Your challenge as a loving parent is to find ways to support desired behavior changes without making your child feel "wrong" for who he or she is.

Very extreme behaviors—such as a complete lack of social interaction, or chronic and violent aggression—may indicate the presence of a biochemical or psychological problem that requires the intervention of a qualified professional. Don't ever be afraid or ashamed to seek such care for your child if you have any suspicion that it might be needed.

Touch your children, hug them, and kiss them. Children (and adults!) thrive when they receive a daily dose of loving touch. Even adolescents secretly love the physical affection they get from their parents (despite what they say!). Positive physical contact has a powerful effect on our children—in fact, babies who are denied this contact will "fail to thrive." Your child has a physical as well as an emotional need for your loving touch.

Say it in words! Don't assume that your children know how much you love them—they need to hear you say it. Don't worry about overdoing it, or sounding mushy—children bask in the glow of being told how important they are, and how much they are loved. You can say "I love you" in many, many ways: "You're so important to me." "I love being with you—you're such good company." "You're a wonderful kid." "I feel so glad to be your mommy." "I'm so lucky to have a girl/boy like you." I tell my kids constantly how much they mean to me, and how much I love them. One day, my daughter Vanessa threw her arms around me, heaved a big sigh, and said, "Mommy, I love you—as much as I could love you!" This has become our regular way of telling each other just how much love there is between us.

When we show our children pure, unconditional love every single day, we build a solid, secure relationship that can weather the fiercest storms. Love is the glue that keeps us together when we make the biggest parenting blunders. Love is the gentle bond that cushions us during the turbulent times in our children's lives (such as adolescence). Love is the main ingredient in building our children's healthy self-esteem. So, take the time today, and every day, to show your children—and tell them in words—that you love them.

Reminder Page—
Building Your Child's Self-Esteem

Choose Your Words Carefully

Think before you speak.

Develop Positive Thinking Skills

Give positive feedback. Discuss positive thinking. Be a positive role model.

Develop Your Children's Best Qualities

Nurture your child's strengths and talents.

Praise and Encourage

Do it—often.

Listen With Your Heart

Listen *actively*: make eye contact, focus on what your child is saying, show that you're listening through words and body language. Validate your child's fears and feelings. Focus on solutions.

Show Love

Use your parenting skills. Accept your child as he or she is. Touch, kiss, hug. Say "I love you" every day, in many ways.

6

How to Nurture
Sibling Relationships

All our early relationships have dramatic effects on our identity, our self-concept, and the choices we make throughout our lifetime. What siblings tell each other, how they treat each other, and the roles assigned each sibling by their parents can have either toxic or beneficial effects on an individual. The more you can consciously treat each of your children as a unique and important person, the greater their chance of growing and developing in harmony with you and each other. If you are a parent of more than one child, understanding the dynamics of sibling connections can help you nurture positive relationships within your family. In addition, if your children relate to each other in a healthy and loving way, you will also find more joy in being a parent.

Realistic Expectations

The first step to gaining peace of mind about sibling relationships is to understand where the rivalry comes from, and to make sure that your expectations are realistic. The rivalry between siblings comes not from their feelings about each other, but from their need to be loved by their parents. It seems that every child wants to be loved most and loved best. Maybe this goes back to ancestral memories of competing for scarce food supplies—but, whatever the source, it is this subconscious competition for Mom and Dad's love, approval, and attention that spurs the battles between children. (In other words, it's *not* because they're wicked, or selfish, or coldhearted.) Any human beings grouped together without choice for long periods of time are bound to have disagreements. Children do not innately have—and should not be expected to have—the skills to settle these disagreements peaceably. Throw into this pot the ever-present demand to share possessions, time, and space, along with every child's less-than-objective notion of fairness, and you can see that sibling rivalry is normal, natural, and inevitable. As a matter of fact, psychologists now feel that sibling conflict isn't necessarily bad. Instead, it can be the fertile ground where children learn valuable social skills relating to compromise, negotiation, and empathy. Perhaps, then, the best route to parental sanity is to expect conflict, understand its roots, manage it when you can . . . and always make sure you have a good pair of earplugs on hand!

Begin at the Beginning

I was lucky enough to begin my study of sibling relationships when I was pregnant with my second child. I believe that having knowledge and a bag full of skills ready for use made having two, and then three, children easier to manage. For the sake of those parents who are just confronting sibling issues, I'd like to share the best ideas for starting off right.

Acknowledge your firstborn's feelings about the new baby. This is especially important during the adjustment period when a new baby is brought home. Instead of saying exclusively Pollyanna-ish things like, "You love the baby," or "You're so lucky to have a baby sister," (which your child may or may not agree with), you can acknowledge your child's difficult feelings: "I know it's hard for you to have to be quiet when the baby's sleeping"; "I bet you wish Mommy didn't have to spend so much time taking care of the baby." Such statements let your child know that his feelings are normal. It's also crucial to make statements that let your older child know that you still love him or her despite the presence of the new sibling: "You are very special to Mommy, and I always love you, no matter how busy I get sometimes with your baby brother."

Don't blame everything on "the baby"! It's so easy to get caught in this trap: "We can't go to the park because *the baby's* sleeping." "I can't play now, I'm giving *the baby* his bath." "Wait until I'm done changing *the baby*." "Be quiet now, *the baby's* sleeping." This is a wonderful way to give sibling rivalry a jump start! Your firstborn will be thinking, "All I ever hear about around here is *the baby*! We can never do anything fun anymore because of *the baby*. I hate *the baby* and I wish she weren't here!" Instead of creating this monster, look for other explanations to give your older child: "I can't right now, *my hands are busy"*; "We'll read *later, after dinner"*; "We'll go to the park *when Daddy gets home"*; or even just, "Not right now."

Avoid saying No, Don't, *and* Stop. These are three words a toddler hears over and over again as soon as a new baby enters the house. Make a commitment to delete them from your vocabulary! There are other ways to handle the situations that initiate these words. For example, one problem that brings about many of these words is the desire of your older child to "touch" the baby, often in not-so-gentle ways. There are two important ways to handle this situation: *hover* and *distract*. First, just hover! Let your older child touch and feel the baby, but be close enough to scoop up the baby and distract your older child. I recently was at a friend's home holding Jennifer, her newborn daughter. Her two-year-old son, Josh, was showing his baby sister the new Big Bird toy I had brought him. The toy inched closer and closer to her face. When the situation looked dangerously close to a poke in the eye, I refrained from yelling, "Stop!" or "No!" Instead I said, "Josh, can I see what color eyes Big Bird has?" Immediately, Big Bird's path was re-directed. If there hadn't been enough time to re-direct the toy, I would have just stood up with the baby in my arms, effectively putting her out of Josh's way. Distraction is actually the skill of choice when it comes to dealing with a toddler's interactions with the new baby. Young children have little understanding of the fact that this little pink squirming object is actually a living, breathing person. No amount of lecturing will impart this knowledge—only time will do that.

The flip side to this technique is to make a positive comment every time the child does something right with the baby. This will reinforce the good behavior. You can make positive comments that will serve to bond the two of them together. "Josh! Jennifer's looking right at you! I think she loves you." "Josh, you touched her so softly. You really know how to touch babies." Incidentally, the best time to let your child touch and hold the baby is when the baby is sleeping. Most babies will sleep through anything—and that includes having big brother put on her socks or stroke her head.

Make sure your older child gets a dose of one-on-one time every day from people he loves—Mommy and Daddy or other important adults in his life. The more your child feels secure in his place in the family, and the more loved he feels, the less likely it is that sibling rivalry will be a problem. Don't, however, make a big deal about this *"special time—just me and you without the baby."* Such comments plant the idea that time between you is special *only* when the baby's not around. Make these times come about naturally, without calling attention to the fact that the baby is being left behind. When each child feels loved and valued, and when each child gets enough attention, sibling rivalry can be brought under control.

Another way to make sure your older child feels she is getting enough time is to give her time *when she wants it*. This is actually very easy to do. When your child says, "Will you play with me?" or "Will you read to me?", say *Yes!* Understand that you do not have to commit hours to your child.

Typically, even four or five minutes of undivided attention will do the trick. What works well is to respond to the request for attention by saying, "Okay. Mommy can play with you for four minutes. I'll set the timer. When it rings, I'll need to go back to doing my work." Then, give your child four minutes of total, undivided attention. When the timer rings, give her a kiss and a hug, and say, "That was fun! Gotta go back to work now." Most often, your child will feel that her "cup has been filled," and she will be able to separate from you easily.

Studies show that the sibling bond is formed at a very young age—even children as young as four months old can develop rapport with their older siblings. These early interactions provide a strong foundation for a lifetime relationship.

Set the Scene for Peace

What's the first word that comes to your mind when I say "Sibling"? Did you happen to think, "Rivalry"? In a recent class, I asked parents to play word association with me, to close their eyes and shout out the first word that came to mind when I said *Sibling*. One hundred percent of the participants shouted *Rivalry!* A roar of understanding laughter followed. When parents have more than one child in the house, their biggest issue is dealing with the way in which the children interact.

Kids fight. Kids bicker. Kids quarrel, argue, and pick at each other. And *it can drive you crazy!* You cannot stop the fighting, but there is much you can do to deal with it, limit it, or at least restructure it into less offensive, more productive activity.

You may be able to control some of the factors that trigger fights between your children. Kids often fight more at certain times of the day, or in certain situations. Take a close look at your family to see if you can determine some of the real reasons your kids are fighting, and then try to find solutions.

Does fighting occur just before dinner? Kids really need to eat more often than three times a day. The stretch between lunch and dinner can be too long for some children. To make matters worse, they have to see and smell the food as you prepare the meal. They are underfoot, picking on each other, and getting in your way. Try feeding the kids a healthy snack at this time since hunger (or high-sugar snacks) can trigger irritability. If pre-dinner irritability is a problem in your home, you may decide that it's worthwhile to feed the kids their dinner at 4:30. This will make it much more likely that you and your spouse can enjoy a quiet meal later on, while the kids join you for conversation and a snack or their dessert.

Boredom can also be a problem during the after-school but before-dinner hour. It helps to have a structured routine or planned activities for this time period. Far too many of us turn to videos or "Sesame Street" for relief during the pre-dinner hour. But there are other, less passive activities that can delight your children and give you enough of a break to make dinner. Play-doh and blocks are old standbys for preschoolers. Quiz your older kids about what activities might keep them happy. (Lucky are the parents who live in neighborhoods that are both safe and filled with children who love to play together outside!)

Does fighting occur just before bedtime? I've heard many parents refer to this as "the Arsenic Hour," or point to a fussy, whiny child and explain, "He's just tired." It's kind of like the weather—everyone talks about it but no one does anything about it! But unlike the weather, you *can* do something about fussy, tired children. It helps to have a very specific routine for the after-dinner hours. When you organize this routine, be sure to include some Mom and Dad time, since many kids, unconsciously, fight to get attention from their parents. There are lots of competing needs at this time of day: parents are trying to get things done, and unwind from the day, at the same time that their children are badly in need of undivided attention. By scheduling time for "family play," you may find that the evening mood lightens considerably. A special bedtime routine that includes time for sharing feelings and thoughts, followed by reading together can be an effective deterrent to late-night fights, and will also encourage family unity. An added bonus is that you strengthen your ability to communicate with your children, and set up a pattern that will help you through the trying adolescent years. If this doesn't feel right for your brood, try the strategy of the father of five sons we mentioned in the last chapter: set aside one-on-one evening time on a regular basis for each parent with each child. What you do or talk about can be determined by the child; the important thing is for your kids to know that they can count on this time together with you.

Do your children fight when they have had too much unstructured time to-gether? When the kids are playing together nicely, we tend to leave well enough alone. But as the time goes on, they get their fill of each other, and begin to bicker and fight. Don't overestimate your children's endurance! Interrupt unstructured playtime before it starts going sour. This is a good time for kids to do homework or household chores, set the table, and help make dinner. Even preschoolers like to help, and appreciate the respect conferred on them by responsibility. If things are going badly, it can save you hours of aggravation to postpone your own chores for five or ten minutes and share some cozy time with your kids: read them a book, set them up with some dancing music, or just sit and give them a hug. This may be all it takes to give everyone a fresh start.

Does fighting occur over the sharing of toys? We want our kids to share. We hate it when they don't. But many parents are without any real plan or method for teaching their kids to share, or for handling the times when they don't. It helps children to have specific guidelines to follow when it comes to sharing. Every family has different ideas about how this should be handled. What's important is that you take the time to decide upon your family rules for sharing. Next, decide on the consequences for not obeying the rules. Keep them simple. Write them down. Post them on the refrigerator at child's-eye level. Illustrate with pictures for young children (stick people work!). Most important: follow through every time.

Don't Be the Family Referee

"Who started it?" and "What happened?" are very dangerous questions. Usually, you don't need to know. Allowing your children to drag you into each and every dispute is unhealthy for their relationship, and frustrating for you. Instead, follow the suggestions in this chapter to put the responsibility and the authority for handling fights right where it belongs—in the kids' hands.

Stand Back and Back Off

The most important rule when it comes to interfering in children's fights is: Don't do it. Most often, if you will just leave the room, your children will work it out without you. If you stick around, one of two things will happen: you won't be able to stand it, and you'll step in the ring; or your children will fight more and longer in an effort to get you to solve their problem, and label someone the winner and someone the loser. You don't need to rush in to solve every problem. Listen for signals that the scene is getting out of hand, but otherwise, don't get involved. The more you manage to stay out of it, the more creative your children will be in solving their own squabbles.

In our home we have used this concept effectively. I realized just how effectively not too long ago:

> *David, age three, and Angela, age seven, were playing with Play-doh at the kitchen table. I was sitting on the floor in the family room folding school newsletters. Suddenly, David and Angela began a verbal battle. I was quietly listening, when David suddenly said something very rude to Angela. I said to him, "David! That was a very unkind thing to say to your sister." As casually as can be, David looked over his shoulder at me and said, "Excuse me, Mommy, but this is between me and Angela. You're in-fer-neer-ing."*
>
> *I was so shocked that I just said, "Oh. Sorry for interfering," and left the room because I could not control my laughter!*
>
> *Now, many parents I know would have said something like, "Don't talk to me that way, young man!" Me? I felt like celebrating. At barely three years old, my son already understood that he and his sister had the ability to work through their problems without my help.*

Sure enough, by the time I returned to the room, the two of them were again playing peacefully together.

Plant the Seeds of Positive Communication

Add to your store of ready phrases such things as, "I know you two can work this out," and "I have confidence that you'll find a solution." There is much to be said for the phenomenon of *self-fulfilling prophecies*. This is the exact opposite of having your children always hear you say, "Can't you two *ever* get along?" or "Why are you *always* fighting?" All your words—as well as your tone of voice, and gestures—will have a dramatic influence on your children's belief system. When they always hear you affirming their ability to get along and find solutions, they will come to believe you.

Make Suggestions and Let the Kids Decide What to Do with Them

If you can see what the problem is, don't jump in with your solution—because whatever your idea is, it won't make everybody happy anyway. Instead, drop a few hints, such as: "Since there are *four* trucks and *two* children, I think you can find a way to share." Then leave the room and let them decide how to solve the problem. For a more complex situation, you can give several ideas, or parts of ideas, and then let your children decide what to do.

For younger children, you can be very specific with your ideas, and even help your kids role-play through the process of negotiation:

Petra, age three, and Pedro, age four, are fighting over a baseball bat and ball. Dad watches for a few minutes to see if they can work it out. As he watches, it is obvious that things are only getting worse, not better. Dad walks over and stands between the two children:

Dad:	Petra, I can see that you want the ball that Pedro has. Say to him, "Pedro, can I have the ball?"
Petra:	Pedro, can I have the ball?
Pedro:	Daddy! It's mine, I want it.
Dad:	Then say to Petra, "It's mine, I want to play with it."
Pedro:	It's mine, I want to play with it.
Dad:	Petra, ask Pedro, "Can we play together?"
Petra:	Pedro, can we play together?
Pedro:	Okay—but I get the mitt.

This may seem kind of silly from an adult perspective, but young children need focused help in learning how to negotiate. And most children from about age two to four will willingly mimic you as you take them through the process. Many parents report great success with this technique. After some practice with you, your children will start using the same format to work things out on their own. One mom reported training her two young children so successfully that one day she was standing in the kitchen and they came running in to say, "Mommy, we have a plan. We each get the wagon for two minutes, but we can't reach the timer. Can you set it for two minutes?"

Discourage Tattling

Kids need to learn that they can handle problems with each other without always running to a parent. We have a rule in our house—unless there's blood or something's broken, I don't need to hear about it! When one of my three children approaches me to tattle, I ask two questions, "Is there any blood? Is anything broken?" If they say no, I respond, "Then I think you can work this out yourself." This usually works very well, except for one day:

Angela:	Mommy! Vanessa took . . .
Me:	(Interrupting her) Is there any blood?
Angela:	No.
Me:	Is anything broken?
Angela:	(A moment of silence) Yes. Our friendship.

Show Positive Attention

When your children are playing together nicely, make it a habit to give them praise and encouragement. It's too tempting to ignore children when they are playing quietly together. It may feel like your one chance to make dinner, or catch up on some paperwork, or just enjoy a minute of peace and quiet! But this is when you really need to stop by, put your arm around your kids, and tell them that you love them, and are so glad they are friends. Because your children crave your attention and approval, your praise will do more to reinforce positive behavior than any amount of scolding. In fact, if scolding is the main sort of attention your kids get from you, it will actually reinforce negative behaviors—because it's still attention, and it's still coming from you. So keep an eye open and your ears cocked for the kind of behavior you want between your children, and take advantage of every opportunity to tell them what a great job they're doing.

Appreciate Children for Who They Are

"Why can't you clean up your room like your sister does?"

"Can't you remember your homework? I never had to remind your brother."

"Don't cry, honey, you're just not as athletic as your sister is."

"You can do that even better than your big brother!"

When we compare our children, it hurts them both. Comparisons breed the jealousy and rivalry we try so hard to control. Children are struggling to find out just who they are, and trying to develop their self-confidence. There is nothing that defeats this process more than being told you are not as good as someone else, especially if that someone else is a peer or a member of your family. Such comparisons also create jealousy and anger toward the peer or sibling who has the admired trait.

Focus on each of your children individually, and appreciate them for who they are. If the bedroom of one of your daughters is always neat as a pin, and your other daughter is as sloppy as can be, avoid saying, "Why can't you be neat like your sister?" Instead, use the other skills presented in this book. *Make a statement*: "Your room is disorganized and cluttered. I have confidence that you can straighten it up." *Use Grandma's Rule*: "When your room is cleaned up, you may join us for a video." *Ask helpful questions*: "What can we do to keep your room neat?"

Fair Does Not Necessarily Mean Equal

"It isn't fair!"

"You gave him more than me!"

"Why can't I have one, too!"

How many times have you heard such expressions of outrage at injustice from one of your kids? Children—again, perhaps out of some ancestral memory of scant resources—are always trying to see that they get their fair share of everything in life. The reality is that life isn't always fair. And when it is, fair doesn't necessarily mean equal. The sooner your children learn this, the happier they will be. Children who never learn this lesson grow up to be adults who cannot find happiness in their lives, because they are too busy moping about their neighbor's new car, their co-worker's new promotion, their friend's new home, and the lady they read about in *Reader's Digest* who won the state lottery.

Teach your children about the richness of differences—the fairness in all of us being different people with differences in our particular needs and wishes; about the beauty of being individuals, and the impossibility of each of us having precisely the same piece of the pie. (Of course, you may also want to teach your children to stand up against unfairness when it's a blatant expression of prejudice, cruelty, or favoritism—but this is another topic for discussion.)

Consider the responses given below to a child's expression of outraged injustice. When stated with a calm, matter-of-fact attitude, such statements can plant the seeds for understanding life's inevitable inequities:

"You gave her more than me!"	"I don't need to hear about your sister. What are your needs?"
"You gave him three sausages, and I only have two!"	"If you're still hungry, just say, 'Mom, may I please have more?'"
"Why didn't you buy me pajamas, too?"	"Because you don't need new pajamas."
"It isn't fair that he gets to stay up later than me."	"Well. Life doesn't always seem fair."
"I *never* get to go with Daddy!"	"I can hear that you really wish you could go with Daddy today."
"You're spending too much time with Becky. I want you to play with me."	"Planning a party does take a lot of time. When Becky and I are done, then you and I can play."

You can help your children focus on their own feelings and needs separately from their siblings' feelings and needs. One crucial thing to point out to your kids, and for you yourself to understand, is that we all have our moment in the spotlight. There are times when one sibling will receive a gift, a compliment, or attention, and the other will not. This is okay! Don't feel that gifts, compliments, and attention must be measured and given out in precisely equal doses at all times. This creates an unnecessary burden on you, and creates an unrealistic view of the world for your children.

One family with three children I know buys *each child* a small gift when one of them has a birthday, so that the other two won't feel left out. This same family makes sure that if someone compliments one of their children, the parents immediately jump in with compliments for the other two. Such attempts at equity are really misguided. Instead of preventing their children, from feeling left out, they are creating an unrealistic worldview in their children—whenever someone gets something, *I* get something, too. What these scrupulously caring parents are failing to see is that the world won't provide for their children in this way—in fact, the world will have some very rude, disillusioning surprises in store for kids raised with such expectations.

It's a far greater favor to your children to encourage them to feel good about their sibling receiving a gift, a compliment, or attention. You can do this by involving the other children in the process. Look at the difference between these two scenes:

Scene One

Uncle Lee: Reiko! You sure read beautifully. (Reiko looks very proud and happy)

Parent: And, look—Midori can sound out all her letters already. (Midori begins to sound out her letters, very loudly; Reiko's face falls)

Scene Two

Uncle Lee: Reiko! You sure read beautifully. (Reiko looks very proud and happy)

Parent: Yes, she sure does. Midori, tell Uncle Lee about how Reiko reads books to you now!

Midori: Reiko reads me Big Bird!

Reiko: (Looking very important) Go get your book, Midori, and I'll read it to you now. (Both children are happy and satisfied)

You can use this same principle when a child receives a gift or special attention. Draw the other sibling into the conversation in a way that includes the one child in the other's glory, rather than setting up a competing focus for attention. Make sure there are times when you purchase something for one child without buying anything for the other. Perhaps it's a school notebook, a pair of pajamas, or a book from their favorite series. When you first do this, expect some complaints from the gift-less child. But if you handle the situation with grace and love, any traces of resentment will fade over time. I know, because I regularly bring home something for one of my three children, and the other two look at the item with interest, but without jealousy. (Of course, make sure that the same child isn't always being left out—this is just asking too much of a child's generosity.)

Encourage Loving Feelings Between Siblings

Make a big deal out of the little things your kids do for each other. Call attention to their acts of love. When one sibling helps another with her homework problem, say, "It's very responsible of you to help your sister." When one child shows concern for another who has been hurt, say, "You're such a loving and caring brother." When one lets the other go first during a game, reinforce this with, "That's kind of you to let your brother go first."

Encourage children to get involved in planning something special for a sibling's birthday or another special occasion. Take them shopping for a gift for their sibling. Stir up the exciting feelings of giving and caring, and teach them about the satisfaction that comes with understanding someone so well that you know just what gift to give. Even when it's not a special occasion, find ways to help siblings show one another their love. Often a suggestion will get your child moving in the right direction. As an example, if you're shopping with one child, and see a favorite treat or trinket of another child, you might say, "Wow! Look at these Batman underwear! Your brother would just love them, don't you think? What if we buy them, and you can surprise him with them when we get home? You're about the only person in the world who knows just how much your brother loves Batman."

Siblings' Day

In our family we have found a great way to celebrate the kids' love for each other. We celebrate "Siblings' Day" (why not—there's Mother's, Father's, Grandparents', and even National Secretary's Day!). We picked the first Saturday in August, since the kids' birthdays fall in October through March. I take them each shopping separately for gifts for each other, we have decorations, cake, and ice cream—the works. During the party, they all promise to always love each other, and take care of each other. It's a very special day for them to focus on their relationship, and a lot of fun, too. With this sort of occasion, you can begin a ritual that will help keep your children close to one another, for the rest of their lives.

Reminder Page—How To Nurture Sibling Relationships

Have Realistic Expectations
Conflict is normal.

Set the Scene for Peace
Use routines and rules. Avoid situations that breed rivalry.

Don't Be the Referee: Stand Back and Back Off
Let them work it out.

Encourage Positive Communication
Keep your words positive. Make suggestions. Discourage tattling.

Show Positive Attention
Appreciate children for who they are.
Don't compare.

Fair Does Not Necessarily Mean Equal
Focus on each child's individual needs.

Encourage Sibling Love
Look for the good. Make comments that build love between your children.

7

Why Do I Get So Angry? How Can I Stop?

Anger. No one wants to talk about it. Everyone feels guilty about it. All parents think they're the *only ones* who get *this* angry at their kids. No one seems to know how to handle it. Yet parental anger is as much a part of parenting as changing diapers. We all do okay with the diapers, yet few of us handle our anger well. It's time we eliminated the guilt, increased our understanding, and learned new skills to handle our anger. Parenting is one of the most time-consuming, energy-consuming, and challenging tasks you will ever encounter, and anger is a natural outcome of the intensity of the work. Rest assured—it happens to everyone!

I teach parenting classes. I have many parenting skills. I have knowledge, and I know how to help parents with their discipline problems. And. . . I am human.

> Picture this. It's 10:30 PM. My three children have invited my sisters' two children to sleep over at our house—only, nobody is sleeping. Only one person *wants* to sleep—and it isn't any of the kids! I've had it. After two hours of *trying* to get the five kids to bed, I finally yell, "Everyone! Get in this bedroom!" I, ever so gently, of course, assist them into the bedroom, bellow, "Now go to sleep!" and firmly pull the door closed.

Okay, not firmly. Wildly. And when I'm done, the doorknob is no longer on the door—it's in my hand!

My mom, who heard the loud "Bang!" of the door, comes out of her room, takes one look at me—my face bright red, my ody tense, the veins sticking out on my neck, and a doorknob in my hand—turns around, and goes back into her room. I hear the unmistakable click as she locks her door!

The day after this horrifying episode, I began my research on parental anger. I figured that if *I* still struggled with it, then many other parents did, too. I was right. When I began to open the door to conversations about anger, using *my* great story as an icebreaker, you wouldn't believe the stories I heard! And parents everywhere shared the same feelings about their anger:

"I hate it when I get so angry."

"I don't know how to stop myself."

"It scares me."

"I just want to scream!"

"I really feel like I lose it."

"Afterwards I feel so guilty and ashamed."

Why Do We Get So Angry?

There are a number of reasons why we get so angry at our children. Understanding the reasons is the first step in gaining control of our angry feelings, and moving toward better solutions. When you understand the reasons for your anger, you can control your feelings just by taking an objective view of the situation. A deeper understanding of what is below the surface can often stop anger in its tracks. So let's take a closer look at the reasons why we get angry at our children.

Lack of Training

Parenting is a 24-hour-a-day job that presents us with constant challenges. Yet most of us have had no parenting training at all! When we first bring home our wonderful child, we quickly discover that there are no attached instructions, and we must struggle through the on-the-job training—with no teacher to help or guide us. Every person must undergo training, pass a test, and get a license to drive a car—but anyone can become a parent with no skills, no knowledge, and no training. Yet raising a child is a life-or-death responsibility; and may be the most important, challenging, difficult, intense, frustrating, exciting job you'll ever have. It is because of our feelings of helplessness, confusion, fear, and frustration that we sometimes erupt in anger.

Children Have Free Will

You cannot *make* a child eat, sleep, listen, move, say please, say I'm sorry, or go potty! Children have free will, and function totally independently of their parents from the moment of birth, even though they're totally incapable of *surviving* independently. It can be so frustrating. Kids are kids. They are not "rational" in the adult sense of the word. Often, we cannot understand what they are doing, or why, because *they* don't understand it themselves. Children are not mini-adults. They have a long way to go before they have the depth of understanding of life to make real sense out of it (then again, some people never do). So, we cannot control our children, but, oh, how we try! When they just won't do it our way, when they don't give a textbook response to the parenting skills we are using with them, when they insist on courses of action that are harmful to them, it's easy to explode in anger.

Our Expectations Differ from Reality

When I was expecting our first child's arrival, I had a vision of what life would be like with a child in our home. I could see us in our cozy home: I'd be watching our child playing and laughing as I baked homemade chocolate chip cookies in the kitchen. Nowhere in my vision did I see myself dismantling the bedroom door in a fit of anger! When our expectations don't match up with reality, it creates frustration and anger. This is true for our overall expectations of family life, just as it is true for any individual situation that occurs. The farther our expectations are from reality, the more room there is for anger.

> Debbie decided to take the day off work to give her two boys an outing at the zoo. She had a vision of a fun family outing and some quality time with her children. The reality couldn't have been farther from her expectations. It started in the car on the way to the zoo. The boys fought over every little thing—"His stuff is on my side of the seat! He's taking my crayons! He's looking at me!" That was just the beginning. As soon as they arrived, Kyle wanted to see the reptiles, and Luke wanted to see the lions—so they fought, until Debbie told them they were going to see the monkeys—and they both got mad at her! She then bought a cotton candy—but the boys complained because they each wanted one of their own. On and on it went, until Debbie cut the day short. The boys cried all the way home, while Debbie fumed over her lost paycheck and a wasted day.

Life Makes Us Angry, and We Take It Out on Our Kids

Consider these two scenarios:

Scene One

You and your partner have a dinner date. Your partner arrives home early, with a bouquet of flowers for you. You leave the kids with a sitter whom they love. You see their sweet faces smiling as they wave to you when you drive off in the car. Your partner whispers sweet nothings all the way to the restaurant. You go to your favorite restaurant, eat a great meal, and enjoy pleasant conversation. The movie you see is "The Bodyguard," a tender love story. When you arrive home, the babysitter is doing her homework, and the kids are peacefully sleeping. The sitter tells you that the kids played peacefully all night, so she took advantage of the time and cleaned up the house for you, and did a few loads of laundry; and her mom's on the way to pick her up, so you don't have to worry about driving her home. As soon as she leaves, you and your partner go hand in hand up the stairs. You enjoy a night of lovemaking, falling asleep in your sweetheart's arms. When you awaken the next morning, your partner has left a note that says, "I love you!" on your pillow. You float down to the kitchen to serve the kids their breakfast. *Your youngest then accidentally spills a whole bowl of cereal all over the table.* You put your arm around your child and gently say, "Don't worry, honey. I'll clean it all up and get you a new bowl. No problem! Everybody has accidents. I sure love you kids."

Scene Two

You and your partner have a dinner date. You're leaving the kids with a sitter, and as you pry your little one's chocolate-covered fingers off your white silk skirt, and try to console your three-year-old who is begging you not to go, your partner is sitting in the driveway laying on the horn. As you drive off, your partner nags at you for being late. You bicker all the way to the restaurant. You go to your favorite restaurant, only to find there's a 45-minute wait for a table. Since you don't have that much time, you grab a burger at McDonald's, which you *so* enjoy (because the kids are collecting the latest Happy Meal prizes, and the idea of another burger really excites you). You head for the movie. "The Bodyguard" is all sold out, so you get to see "Rambo Fights Godzilla." Your partner's in a lousy mood, and you fight on the way home. When you arrive home, the babysitter is asleep, but the kids are still up. They're in the livingroom in front of the TV, eating a whole box of cookies and a bag of chips, the remains of which are all over your furniture and carpeting. Your partner takes the sitter home, then goes to bed. By the time you get the kids to sleep, your partner is snoring. When you awaken the next morning, you can tell your partner has left for work by the mess left in the bathroom. You drag yourself down to the kitchen to serve the kids their breakfast. *Your youngest then accidentally spills a whole bowl of cereal all over the table.* You yell, "You klutzy kid! Look at this mess! Move out of the way. You kids seem to think I'm your maid. I'm sick and tired of cleaning up after you. That's all I ever seem to do around here, clean up after everybody else. . . ."

The spilled bowl of cereal was *not* what caused your angry feelings! Your lousy dinner date with your partner, the messy bathroom, and your overall unhappiness were, in fact, the real cause. It helps to understand that, at times, the anger we take out on our children has nothing to do with them at all. And when we can learn to separate the two, we are on our way to controlling our feelings. (More about *how to do this* later.)

Anger Masks Other Emotions

Your adolescent is due home by his 10:00 PM curfew. It's 10:30—you're upset that he's late. By 11:00, you are furious that he's so late. It's 11:30, and you are starting to worry and wonder where he is. By 11:45, you are scared to death. At 11:50, your child walks in the front door and says, "Hi! Sorry I'm late."

You . . . hug and kiss him and say, "I was so worried about you. I'm glad you're safe!" No way. You scream, "You are *two hours* late, young man. You know the rules! Where have you been? Get up to your room. You are grounded for the next two weeks!" *Anger* is only the presenting emotion in this situation, even though *fear* and *relief* are the underlying emotions.

Often, our anger is masking other emotions such as fear, frustration, pain, embarrassment, confusion, or stress. This happens as a matter of course—the anger saves us from having to experience the pain of the other emotions. Although it's difficult to be able to feel those painful emotions as they occur, you'll make considerable progress if you can just acknowledge to yourself that they are there.

Anger Is a Natural, Normal Human Emotion

Part of being human is having a wide range of emotions. Anger is unpleasant, but it is both normal and natural. Anger makes its first appearance when a new baby enters the world red-faced and screaming!

Most people don't want to be caught in public angry any more than they want to be caught in public in their underwear. It is easier to get angry with those closest to us, because we feel less vulnerable, and freer to "let down our guard." And because we spend a large proportion of our time under the same roof as our children, there are many opportunities for anger to make an appearance in family relationships. Our most intimate bonds are also those most likely to spark fear, frustration, pain, embarrassment, confusion, and stress—which we may try to escape by feeling angry instead.

Although anger is normal, people handle it in a wide variety of ways. Although no one can avoid being angry ever, we *can* learn to control our personal response to our anger, and how to direct it in more productive ways.

Two Levels of Anger

There are two different levels of anger. At one level, you may feel annoyed, irritated, upset, aggravated, bothered, or disturbed—but you can still think rationally. Your anger may cause you to become very focused and assertive. This can actually be a productive state of mind. Psychologists call this "controlled anger." We understand what is causing our anger, and we deliberately act in response to the situation. Controlled anger is a very powerful emotion, and it can be used in helpful ways. Dr. Martin Luther King, Jr., Mahatma Gandhi, and the creators of such programs as MADD (Mothers Against Drunk Drivers) and DARE (Drug and Alcohol Resistance Education) have proven the potent effect of controlled anger. Parents can use controlled anger to keep their children on their toes:

> May is standing in the front yard talking with a neighbor. Her two-year-old, Matthew, is playing nearby. Suddenly, Matthew darts out into the street. May runs after him, picks him up firmly, looks him in the eye, and says in a very stern voice, "Matthew! *No street.* It's dangerous! Stay by Mommy."

> Scott, a third grader, recently received a Nintendo computer game for his birthday. He has been obsessed with it to the point of consistently "forgetting" to do his homework. Scott is normally a very responsible kid, and gets good grades in school. Today, however, Scott's father gets a phone call from his teacher. She asks about the letter she sent home regarding Scott's recent neglect of his homework. Scott's father never received the letter. He says he will handle the problem with Scott. That afternoon, when Scott returns home from school, he and his father discuss the problem. They set up a schedule for both homework and Nintendo. As a consequence for failing to give the teacher's letter to his father, and for neglecting his homework, Scott loses his Nintendo privileges for the next week, and he must write a letter explaining his new schedule to his teacher.

In both of these situations, the parents were able to function at a controlled level of anger, with good end results. There are times, however, when we pass into the next level of anger. We may feel exasperated, furious, wild, intense, frantic, violent, or frenzied. At these times we no longer *act*—instead we *react*. We pound the table, slap our child, scream, or pull off a doorknob! Our anger shuts off the "thinking" part of our mind, and we move into the more primitive fight-or-flight mode. We then react in senseless ways, and say and do things that we don't mean. This is hurtful anger, and it interferes with successful parenting. It clouds our view of options, so that the only answer we see to a problem is to wring our kid's neck!

When we are in a stage of hurtful anger, our tendency is to direct the anger at *our child*, rather than at *his behavior*. We use such phrases as: *You always . . . , you never . . . , you are such a . . . , you make me. . .* In other words, we give our child the message, "You are bad." "You are the problem." Hurtful anger creates bad feelings for both the parent and the child. Typically, after an angry outburst, parents feel guilty: they can see that in reality, their anger did not bring about positive results. The child feels resentful and angry—in essence, *your* anger shuts off the thinking portion of *your child's* mind. When your child is immersed in resentful thoughts, he or she is unable to see the problem in a realistic way. Your anger does little to motivate your child towards self-discipline.

Anger, when it is out of control, only causes emotional problems all around, and impedes the learning process that can teach our children how to make better life decisions.

Ways of Thinking That Make Matters Worse

When you are in a state of hurtful or uncontrolled anger, the thoughts running through your head are probably inaccurate (as opposed to rational), and may be based on mistaken beliefs. We tend to see a situation as final and definitive, rather than recognizing it as part of a process. Let's take advantage of your current peaceful state of mind to examine some typical negative thinking a parent might get caught up in while angry, and to discuss each statement from a rational point of view.

"My Kids Should Not Misbehave"

Let's face it. Your kids will misbehave. My kids will misbehave. All kids misbehave. Any child that does not misbehave is . . . well . . . I don't know— I've never seen one! The process of dealing with misbehavior is one of the main functions of parenting. In other words, children learn to a great extent by trial and error—with the emphasis on error. No child is born knowing all the rules of etiquette and good behavior. Learning about these is a process. During this process our children will test all the rules—family rules, society's rules, and rules of nature. It is our job as parents to guide our kids during this process: to teach them right from wrong, and help them move toward adulthood, giving each developmental stage its due.

It is not our children's misbehavior that makes us angry. We make ourselves angry by the way we think about our children's behavior. You might want to post this somewhere:

It is not my children's misbehavior that causes my anger. I cause my own anger by the way I think about and react to their misbehavior.

You may feel overwhelmed at the moment when you are dealing with your child's misbehavior, but remember that all kids misbehave, and all parents have to deal with the misbehavior. It is important that you understand child development to the extent that you can pinpoint certain behaviors as normal. For instance, if you know that two-year-olds are prone to temper tantrums because of their struggle for autonomy and independence, you will find it easier to handle than if you think it's just *your child acting like a brat.* If you understand that adolescents are going through rapid physical, cognitive, and psychological changes, you'll be better equipped to handle their rebellious behaviors.

When a stranger is staring at you when your child is having a temper tantrum in the middle of a store, you can be fairly certain that one of three things is bound to be true: that person doesn't have children, and couldn't possibly understand; that person does have children, and is hoping to learn something from watching how you handle the situation; or the person is thinking, "Sure glad it's him (or her) and not me this time watching my kid lose it completely in public!"

My kids should not misbehave is a mistaken belief. It will help you control your anger if you replace this belief with more rational statements of fact:

All children misbehave.

My child is going to learn something from this experience.

This is the *error* part of trial and error.

My kid is normal. This is typical behavior.

I can handle this.

This too shall pass.

Write these or other rational comebacks on a 3x5 card you can carry in your pocket or purse, and whip it out whenever you hear yourself begin to rehearse mistaken beliefs in you head. Allowing your negative, irrational thoughts to flourish will only feed your anger. Replacing them with more rational statements of fact will allow you to act rather than react to your child's misbehavior.

My very active two-year-old son was quite a handful. When I found that my husband, my mom, or I were getting tense with him, I would lighten up the mood by whispering to the adult, "Hey, David! Grow up! Act your age! Don't be such a baby!" We would then laugh, as we realized that *he was!*

"My Kids Are Acting This Way Just To Make Me Mad"

It sure seems that way sometimes, but let's have a reality check here. Do you honestly think your daughter plans her behavior just to see if she can get you mad enough to cancel her sleep-over party? Or that your two children conspire to see who can get Dad angry enough to hit them? Or that your son's goal is to make you send him to his room for the weekend? Kids hate to see their parents angry. They don't like to deal with the consequences of your anger. They do, however, crave your attention (even your *negative* attention), and they are constantly trying to figure out the rules of the game—which may mean testing the limits of your patience and tolerance. A child who feels a need for attention may know *subconsciously* that certain misbehaviors will get you angry enough to leave whatever you're doing, and give your total undivided attention to your child. In terms of limit testing and trying to figure out the rules, children "push our buttons" to see if they can get their way, or get us to change our mind. The causes of misbehavior are sometimes much simpler and much less goal-oriented: your child may be trying so hard to get you to understand her point of view, and may feel so passionate about it, that *her own* emotions are getting in the way of rational behavior. Simple frustration may be the culprit. So, with these thoughts in mind, try to understand your child's misbehavior, focus on the problem at hand, and decide upon a solution. (There will be more about this later in the chapter.)

"My Kids Know Better"

Come on, is this really true? Not surprisingly, the answer is *yes*. Children are masters at testing the rules and testing their parents to see if they can push the boundaries. Often, our children *do* know better, but they want to find out if the rules still hold true, or if they can get away with something. This is frequently the case with children whose parents are *not* consistent. Such children figure out that if they test a rule, they just might get away with breaking it. This encourages them to test again and again and again. (Remember the gambler at the slot machine? He keeps pulling the lever, hoping to hit the jackpot. All the other pulls are worth it, because the win feels so good.) Even in a family in which the rules are consistently enforced, children will still test to see if a given rule is still in effect, or has for some reason changed. So, yes, our children may know better—but that doesn't mean that they will always follow the rules. You know the speed limit, but do you *always* obey it? Adults, as well as children, may indeed break the rules if they feel they have a good enough reason, a chance of getting away with it, or are simply in the mood to do so.

So the moral to this story is: don't beat yourself up over a normal and natural childhood enterprise. You don't have to *like* it, but neither do you have to give it more of your time and energy than it deserves.

"People Think I'm a Bad Parent When My Kids Act This Way"

Let's go back to our previous example of the kid having a tantrum in the store. The first spectator—the one who doesn't have kids—*is* thinking some pretty judgmental thoughts just now. Try to keep in mind that his or her thoughts have no effect on who you are or what kind of parent you are (unless you change your behavior based on what you think someone else is thinking about you). Keep your priorities straight: what's most important now is to stay rational, and handle your child's tantrum with all your best parenting skills. This isn't the moment to be competing in imaginary popularity contests. The spectators who *are* parents may have the empathy to understand your pain; or, then again, they may also be judgmental, simply because their point of view is necessarily limited, and they don't understand the whole situation. Unless these people are more important to you than your relationship with your child, you'll just have to ignore them.

> One day, I took my three children to the zoo. We didn't have a stroller with us, so we rented one. I guess you could call it a stroller—it was actually a large green plastic dolphin on wheels. David, then two years old, fell in love! But so did Vanessa, then four, and Angela, six. So, being the fair and reasonable mother I am, I announced that David would ride in the stroller most of the time, but Angela and Vanessa would each have a turn. David was one happy camper . . . until it was Vanessa's turn to have a ride. First I had to pry his little fingers off the edge of the stroller, pull his little feet from under the rim, and drag him out of it! Then he pounded his feet on the ground and proceeded to act his age in a full-blown-as-only-a-two-year-old-can-do-it tantrum. I took a deep breath, my eyes sweeping the surrounding spectators, and said, "Come on, David," and proceeded to walk forward. He then threw himself to the ground and continued his show. (I felt like selling tickets and popcorn!) I took a deep breath, walked over to David, picked him up, carried him under my arm (in the football hold), and walked ever so calmly forward with a kicking, screaming two-year-old on my hip. Talk about dirty looks! Those

spectators probably thought I was the worst mother in the world. (I figured that it wouldn't be a good time to pass out brochures for my parenting classes.)

The reality is that I used good parenting skills handling David at the zoo. If I had given in to his tantrum, and let him have exclusive use of the stroller, I would have been setting myself up for many more public tantrums. Instead, it was one of those times when I just had to grit my teeth and teach the lesson. It helps to focus on what's most important—the opinions of strangers, or my relationship with my children? Remember—no matter how many skills you have, you will never have perfect children, nor will you ever be the perfect parent! (Maybe you'd better read that last sentence again.) In fact, there's no such thing as a perfect parent, any more than there's any such thing as a perfect human being.

The rest of the story is that Angela took pity on me, or David, or herself. She put her hand on her little brother's head, and said, "That's okay, David. You can have my turn in the stroller." (She, being the big sister, could get away with this. I, being the mother, could not.) Thank you, Angela, thank you.

"My Children Act This Way Because I'm a Bad Parent"

Mothers are especially good at this line of thinking. Even in our progressive times, the message to women who happen to be mothers is that they are only as good as their children. As proof of this, answer the question, What do you call a mother who works outside the home? A working mother, right? Well, what do you call a father who works outside the home? A man with a job? A lawyer, a plumber, a teacher? The mother is still, for the most part, considered the primary parent, and, as such, is seen as primarily responsible for her children's behavior—even if her husband is a stay-at-home dad. This leaves no room for women who are mothers to have bad days or even bad moments.

When mothers, or fathers, measure their self-worth based on their child's behavior, it's all too easy to feel personally threatened by episodes of misbehavior. Parents caught in this way of thinking may have trouble achieving the distance and sense of separateness required to take action rather than react to what their children say and do. It also makes it hard for children to develop the separate sense of self they need in figuring out just who they are—and who they *aren't*. This problem is demonstrated in the common analogy comparing children to clay—they are formed into a finished product by their parents. Hogwash! I have three children, close in age, same parents, same home, same school; yet they are as different as day, night, and afternoon! I think a better analogy than the traditional "clay" story would go something like this:

Children are like seedlings. Some are like apple trees, some orange, some maple. Some may be more like tomato plants or rosebushes. Parents are like gardeners. They must water, weed, and tend to their young plants. They must know when to support the young plant with a stick, or protect it with a jar. A good parent, like a good gardener, can help a plant become healthy, vibrant, and full of fruit. But a parent, like a gardener, cannot change an apple tree into a maple tree, or a tomato plant into a rosebush.

Our children have free will. We can guide them, nurture them and teach them. But we can never totally own them, nor would we want to. There are times when our children will do things that surprise us, touch us, or anger us. It is all part of the fact that they are separate from us, and, as such, are in the process of growing into mature individuals.

"The Only Way My Kids Listen To Me Is When I Yell"

This may very well be true if you only mean business when you yell. Oftentimes, parents get into the trap of using empty words until they work themselves up into an angry state in which they can't take the misbehavior anymore. They communicate this sense of purpose to their children through anger. After asking a child to do something three times, they finally yell, "I mean it!" (I often wonder why they just didn't mean it the first time!) Witness this:

John is doing paperwork at the kitchen table. His two children, Tina and Will, are playing in the family room. They begin to argue over a toy. John calls from the table, "Come on, guys, I'm trying to work." A few minutes later, the noise level increases. John says, "Kids! I'm working in here." Of course, the noise continues, and John looks up from his work and announces, "I'm starting to get angry!" Soon, the family room erupts with a loud and rowdy game. John, suddenly at his boiling point, charges into the family room, pounds the table with his fist, and shouts, "I've had it! I'm trying to work! Either stop the noise or go to your room and play!" The kids are suddenly quiet. John shakes his head as he wonders why he must get so angry before they listen.

Let's examine John's dilemma. He makes his first three statements from another room with no specific call to action. (I mean, what exactly does "Come on, guys, I'm trying to work" mean?) It isn't until he's angry that he actually uses some good skills! One—he walks into the room, and faces his children directly. Two—he gives them a choice they both can live with—play quietly or leave. In essence, it's not his anger that solved the problem, it's his positive parenting skills. But these are masked by the anger. If John consistently uses this approach, the kids will learn to know that he doesn't mean business until he's angry. If John used his parenting skills right off the bat, without mixing them up with his anger, he would give his children the message that his words matter, even when spoken calmly and cheerfully.

Once you become aware of some of the things you say to yourself that contribute to your anger and frustration, you can move on to the next step: learning specific skills to use when you feel yourself getting angry. When you have a *plan* for dealing with your anger, it will be less overwhelming, and will dissipate sooner. Let me tell you this—since I researched and wrote my lecture called "Managing Parental Anger," the doorknobs in our home have been safe and sound. What's more, I really don't get into that state of "hurtful anger" anymore. Other parents have reported that these skills have made a major difference for them as well. Let's look at the four steps to staying calm.

Four Steps To Staying Calm

Step 1—Stop, Breathe, Count

Stop

There are many stages that lead up to full-blown anger. You can learn to recognize and acknowledge these stages in yourself. Every person is different, but here are some of the common signs of anger: rapid breathing, tightening of the stomach, contracting of the muscles, sweating, shaking, the desire to hit or yell. When you recognize any of these signs of impending anger, you can say to yourself: "**Stop!** I'm getting angry." You can then put space between yourself and your child. This might involve putting a child in a safe place for time out, or putting *yourself* in a safe place for a time out! It is critically important that, when you feel the anger rising in you, you don't try to deal with the situation. You desperately need to put some space between you and your child so that you can get control of yourself—so you will be able to act rather than react.

This is a crucial first step. By making a decision to stop your anger early in the process of feeling yourself get angry, it becomes possible to defuse your anger before it becomes dangerous. Putting space between yourself and your child accomplishes two things: it communicates your anger to your child, and it gives you time when you most need it to calm yourself down before dealing with the situation that is making you angry.

You need to keep in mind that, as a parent, you do not need to have an immediate response to every action, an immediate answer to every question, an immediate consequence for every misbehavior. The advantage in dealing with children—as opposed to, say, a dog or a horse—is that even very young human beings can link two events separated by time. You can't very well say to your dog when he's dragged the Thanksgiving turkey onto the floor, "You're going to be punished for that, Fido, as soon as I calm down enough to think of appropriate consequences." Or you can say it, but you can't realistically hope that Fido will link your punishment with the deed. Whereas even a two-year-old has enough long-term memory and knowledge of causality to allow you to effectively administer some disciplinary action, even if it's somewhat delayed. (If you don't believe me, try telling a two-year-old that you'll take him out for ice cream after dinner—see if he remembers!)

Just recently, I had an opportunity to practice this technique with my seven-year-old daughter. I was dressing to leave for a lecture, and my three children were keeping me company in the bathroom. Angela was playing with her cat's cradle string, but when I looked up, she was twirling it over her head (like a lasso!). I told her to stop, that with all of us in the room, it was dangerous. A few moments later, she was *again* twirling her string, and I told her to stop. You guessed it—a few moments later, she was doing it again. (Hey! She's a healthy, normal seven-year-old just testing the limits.) This twirl landed the string right in her sister's eye. Vanessa's eyelid immediately swelled up and turned red. I was furious (not to mention scared!). I looked at Angela, my face red, my eyes daggerlike, and yelled, "Get out of here!" Angela, being a very smart kid, ran as fast as her little legs could carry her. I tended to Vanessa, putting ice on her eye; determined that there was no eye damage, and calmed her down.

Only then, after calming *myself* down, and after making a decision about an appropriate consequence, did I feel I was ready to confront Angela. I went to her room, and asked her some helpful questions: "What happened when you didn't listen to Mom?" "Why do you suppose I make the rules that I do?" "How do you think Vanessa felt when your string struck her in the eye?" After we explored the answers to these questions, I asked for her cat's cradle string, and told her that she could have it back in three days. She turned it over without a fuss. (For the next three days, though, all I heard was how *bored* she was, and if she could just have her string. . . .)

I would like to point to what I did next as a critical step in maintaining a healthy, loving relationship with your child. I put my arm around my sweet daughter, looked her in the eye, and said, "Honey, even when you don't listen to me, even when you misbehave, I love you with all my heart. You are my one and only Angela, and you're very special to me." She looked up at me, and very earnestly said, "Mommy, I promise I'll never misbehave again."

Let's get back to our steps for staying calm. First, you need to recognize that you're angry, and put some space between you and your child. What you do with that time and space is very important. Don't talk yourself into a frenzy by rehashing the problem and focusing on how mad you are! Try instead to:

Breathe

Once there is space between you and your child, you can take a few deep breaths. Fill your lungs with air, then exhale with a sigh. Taking a few deep breaths helps the physical aspects of anger dissipate. Getting oxygen to your brain and muscles helps your body relax. When we are angry, we tend to take shallow, short breaths, and deny our muscles and brains the oxygen they need to function properly. The process of slow breathing also helps you get your emotional self under control.

Count

Of course you have heard this one many times before—probably because it works! Count—slowly and purposefully—to 10 or 20 (or, if it's *really* bad, go on all the way up to 100). The process of counting takes your mind off the immediate problem, and helps refocus your energy. It also gives you a few minutes to escape from the problem, and calm yourself down before facing it. Some people find that counting is too easy and rote, and doesn't really distract them enough from their anger to calm down. In that case, try reciting the National Anthem, or a complex poem or verse, or song lyrics; or mentally compose your grocery shopping list (heck, make good use of the time and write down your list!). Any of these delaying tactics uses the same principle of giving yourself the mental distance you need to pause and regroup.

You can use the stop, breathe, count sequence even in public places. The only piece of the "stop" segment you must leave out is the part about giving yourself space—although I know of one creative mother who managed to use this part of the process, too! Here's her story:

> Diane* was picking up her three children from swimming lessons.
> As they were getting into the car, the two girls began to argue
> over the seating arrangement in the car (a unique problem). Diane
> stepped in and said, "Julie, sit in the back; Emily, sit in the front."
> Julie, unhappy with the outcome, began a typical 12-year-old act
> of rebellion. She stood in the parking lot, arms folded over her
> chest, face pulled firmly into a pout, and announced, "Then I'm
> not getting into the car." After a few minutes of argument between
> Diane and Julie, Diane felt herself slipping into a dangerous state
> of anger. She stopped, breathed, counted—and calmly got into the
> car, and drove away . . . leaving a very shocked Julie standing in
> the parking lot! (Diane called her husband at work from the car
> phone and asked that he pick up their daughter from the pool
> on his way home from work.)

Now, I don't recommend leaving your child at the scene of the crime—but this story had the whole class in tears, we were laughing so hard!

Step 2—"See" Yourself

Now that you've taken the time to stop, breathe, and count, you are most likely in a better frame of mind to view the situation. Pretend that you're

---

* The names have been changed to protect the guilty.

watching yourself on TV, or, better yet, on a video that you can rewind and fast-forward. You may be surprised to see that you are about to wring your kid's neck because she won't eat her broccoli!

When you see yourself from a more objective point of view, you can often get a better grip on the situation and make some decisions about your behavior before you confront your child. Making the effort to see yourself as an outsider can clarify your long-term objective of helping your child grow through this situation, rather than allowing you to focus exclusively on the short-term clash of wills that is occurring. Seeing yourself helps you get past your angry emotions, so that you can better parent your child. To demonstrate just how powerful this idea is, think about how easy it is to analyze your sister's or your neighbor's parenting mistakes, or the obvious insensitivity of the harried mom in the grocery store! Seeing yourself from the outside lets you take your ego out of the process, and get some perspective on a situation.

Step 3—Adjust Your Expectations

We set ourselves up for high levels of anger by harboring unrealistic expectations. The farther our expectations stray from reality, the more room there is for anger to escalate. Here's an illustration to show how this works, using my sleep-over disaster as the example:

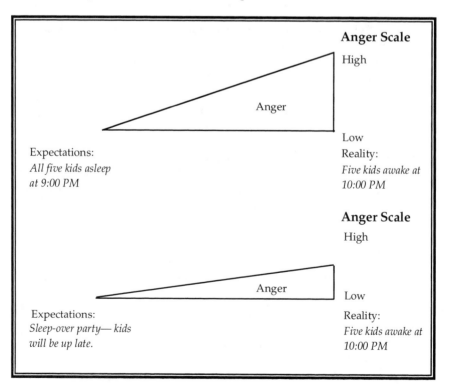

Realistic expectations allow for the misbehaviors that make us angry. When they occur, they don't take us by surprise. You may even have a plan worked out beforehand for dealing with them. Keeping your expectations realistic helps you deal with life as it is, rather than dwelling on how you'd like it to be (and blaming your kids for spoiling your pretty picture). This may be the most important point in this chapter. You can reduce your anger if you understand that parenting is *a process.* This will help you focus on the big picture: the process of helping your children reach adulthood, rather than agonizing over each daily issue that doesn't go according to plan.

It is also critically important to become at least a little knowledgeable about child development, so that you can recognize the times when your children are "just acting their age." That's when your battery of skills can come into play for coping with typical behaviors for each stage of childhood. One of the best series of books available to parents to help them understand the stages of childhood are those by Louise Bates Ames, Ph.D., and colleagues, from the Gesell Institute of Human Development: *Your One-Year-Old, Your Two-Year-Old,* and so on, up to *Your Fourteen-Year-Old.* Each book focuses on the normal development issues for children at that specific age. It can really help to know that *all* seven-year-olds get defiant and sulky, and will cry at the drop of a hat, when you are caught in the middle of it with your seven-year-old! The more you know about normal behavior for a child at a specific age, the more relaxed you can be when situations arise that are just "healthy development." This will keep your expectations realistic, and allow you to avoid anger caused by a lack of understanding on your part of your child's developmental milestones. When your child acts in an expected manner, you can then say to yourself, "Oh! I remember reading about this." Of course, knowledge will neither eliminate the behavior, nor your displeasure in it, but it will allow you to see it for what it is, and deal with it in a more relaxed manner.

When adjusting your expectations, try to keep focused on the *reality* of the problem at hand. Most things that we get so very angry over today, we won't even *remember* three weeks, let alone three years, from now. I just saw a bumper sticker that read, "Don't sweat the small stuff"; and in small letters beneath that, it said, "It's *all* small stuff."

Step 4—Use Skill

In review: you have *stopped, separated, breathed, counted, watched yourself on TV, and adjusted your expectations.* All this may have taken a few minutes or an hour, depending on the intensity of the situation. Now is the time to analyze the situation and decide which skill to use to bring everything under control.

As an example, when my five darlings were up at 10:30, bouncing off the walls, I could have:

- Made a statement: "It's 10:30 and past your bedtimes. Everyone must lie down quietly."

- Given them a choice: "You can all lie quietly in here, or I will find separate sleeping places for everyone."

- Used Grandma's Rule: "When you are all in bed quiet, I will read one book before I turn out the light."

- Made it brief: "Kids—in bed!"

- Made something talk: "Hi! I'm the sleep fairy. When you are in bed with your eyes closed, I will sprinkle you with magic sleep dust, and give you wonderful dreams."

- Written a note: I could have sent a paper airplane into the room with a note attached that said:
  It's way past ten,
  Better get in bed,
  Before your mother
  Turns bright red!

- Used humor: I could have walked into the room, collapsed on the floor pretending to cry, as I said, "Oh, I must get sleep—I'm fading away! I must sleep!"

- Ignored them: "Listen, kids—I'm going to bed. Stay in this room. Stay quiet. And don't bug me."

- Used dramatics: Pulled off a doorknob. (Wait a minute! This isn't a *skill!!*)

Once you have made a decision about what skill to use, with at least one other as a backup, you can then face your child with a different attitude: one that says, "I am the parent. I am in charge. This is the plan." Having a plan will enable you to address the situation in a calm, productive manner.

With practice, you may find that following these steps to staying calm may actually help you avoid getting angry in the first place. But even if you do get mad, your anger will not feel out of control, and you'll have a plan for dealing with it.

Reminder Page—
Why Do I Get So Angry? How Can I Stop?

Steps to Staying Calm

Step 1

- Stop

- Put space between you and your child

- Breathe

- Count

Step 2

"See yourself" on TV.

Step 3

- Adjust your expectations

- Adjust your thinking

Step 4

Choose the skill you'll use; have a backup.

8

How Can You Take Care of Everyone Else If You Don't Take Care of Yourself?

You have just boarded an airplane. A voice on the P.A. system narrates while the flight attendant demonstrates the use of the safety equipment on board the plane. As the attendant holds up the air mask, the voice says, "In the event of a loss in cabin pressure, an oxygen mask will drop from the ceiling above your seat. Pulling down on the air mask will begin the flow of air. Immediately assist your children with their masks. Then assist your spouse with his or her mask. After that, look behind you for any elderly or confused people, and help them with their masks. Double-check the people seated in the row across from you to be certain that their masks are secure. After following these steps, if you have any energy left, put a mask over your own face and gasp for air."

Sound ridiculous? Many parents go about their daily life in just this way, making sure that their children, spouses, parents, friends, neighbors, and the PTA are all taken care of before they will take even a moment for themselves. Noble as it may seem, neglecting your own emotional and physical needs can leave you feeling angry, stressed, resentful, irritable, short-tempered, or sad. Research shows that this kind of lifestyle can lead to more serious problems such as depression and illness. It is important to your entire family for you to take better care of yourself. Let me suggest that

You will be a better parent, a more loving spouse, a more efficient employee or boss, a more patient softball coach, a friendlier friend, an overall better **person** *if you will take time every day, just for you.*

You may be thinking—"Nice thought, but she's *got* to be kidding! The house, the kids, my job—how in the world am I going to find time for myself?" We do live in a very busy world, and we do have many obligations. Trust me—speaking strictly from experience—I understand! I decided some time ago that running from morning to night at high speed was not only wearing me out—it was putting extra pressure on my most important relationships, and taking a toll on my personality. I took a good, hard look at my life and decided: something has got to go! I kept a notebook handy, and made a note anytime I did something that could possibly be done by someone else, something that could be done more easily, more quickly, or more efficiently, or something that I could live without. I was amazed that such little changes could add up to such a big chunk of time! Here are some ideas.

Relax Your Housekeeping Standards, and/or Get Help

Many housework activities can be modified to save time. Just be more creative and give it some real thought. Do you *really* need to fold the bath towels? Or will a heap in a laundry basket in the closet be just as effective? Take a good look at what you're doing, and ask yourself, "Is this really necessary?" Are you bathing the kids every night? Unless they've been playing in the mud, every other night (or dare I suggest every third night?) will do just fine. Do you really need to change the sheets every week, or will every other week do just as well? Pulling out the big vacuum all the time? What about using a small hand-vacuum in between a two-week total vacuum? Picking up the kids' toys all day? Try limiting the amount of toys in any area, and providing lots of labeled boxes for easy cleanup.

When you cook a pot of soup, chili, or spaghetti sauce, make enough for several meals and freeze the extra. How about picking one night a week as "Pizza Night" or "Cereal Night"? One creative mom I know lets each of her four kids make dinner one night a month (the other three have cleanup duty). The kids have a blast, and Mom gets a few nights off from cooking. Does packing lunches take too much energy in the morning? Why not pack the whole week's worth, bag them, and stock them in the refrigerator? Another good idea is to store a tub of cleaning supplies in the rooms where they are needed (just make sure they're out of reach of your children). When you have the supplies handy that you need to clean each bathroom, you may find a few minutes when you can clean up—for example, when the kids are in the bathtub.

Rolling socks? Try piling them in everyone's drawers, and letting each person find his own pair each morning. (My sister read this and laughed. She said it was a great idea for creating more stress in her already harried morning routine. She could imagine the havoc it would create in her house— "Mom!!! I can't find any socks, and I'm late for school!" "Honey! Where are all my socks? All I have is this big pile of *stuff* in my drawer!") Which leads me to remind you not to try *everything* I suggest. Just pick the ideas that will work for you and your family, and maybe think up and try a few of your own.

Have you ever considered hiring a housekeeper to do the main cleaning? If it's not in your budget to hire a pro, how about that teenager down the street who would love a few extra dollars a week? How about your little sister who is saving money for her next vacation? Perhaps you can get some help with just a few time-consuming tasks, like doing the laundry, washing the windows, or waxing the floors. Be creative, and you can spend much less time on housework.

You will, of course, have to relax your standards a bit; but a few years from now that will change: the house will be perfectly clean and tidy, and very, very quiet. And after all, 20 years from now, who's going to remember how clean your toilets were? But 20 years from now, those extra hours will reap great rewards in your relationships with your spouse and kids. What's most important?

Cut Down on TV Time

Take a good look at how much TV your family is watching. You may be surprised to learn that you're spending more time in front of the tube than you thought you were. This kind of time passes quickly, and may be making you or your kids unavailable for quality personal time. Often, people sit down to watch a favorite show, and get hooked into watching one or two more just because the set is on. Make decisions about what program you want to watch, and plan an activity that will occur right after it is over. (This is excellent modeling for your children's benefit!)

Say "No" When You Need To

Look closely at what you are doing for other people. Think carefully before committing to any new activities. You will be surprised at how easily people will accept a simple *No* from you. Women often have trouble with this, because we're taught early on that we're valued for our helpfulness and nurturing qualities. But you can't nurture the whole world. Practice saying, "I'd love to, but I just don't have the time." Often we get involved in activities just to fill someone else's need. Don't be a pushover! Your needs, your priorities, and your energy level are important!

Try "Trip-Chaining"

Take a look at your travel time. People waste a lot of time in the car "doubling back." Try to run errands all at once and in a direct route. Transportation planners call this "trip-chaining." Sometimes it even makes sense to spend a few extra dollars at the closest drycleaner, drugstore, or grocery store, rather than taking that extra 20 minutes to go to the best-priced store. (Calculate your gas, car wear and tear, your time, energy, and attitude, too!)

Use Routines to Make Your Life Easier

Use routines whenever possible to manage impulses, and organize your life. It's amazing how efficiently you can get yourself and everyone else out the door in the morning if you are all following a specified routine. Chaos ensues when everyone is operating on a different wavelength every morning. Routines can also ease the bedtime hours into a smooth-running operation. For these times, a poster or chart with all the details outlined in a simple, easy-to-follow manner can keep everyone organized. Standard routines for daily chores such as homework, dishes, and toy cleanup can keep the family on a calm, even keel. For instance, if homework is always done as soon as the dinner dishes are complete, you will prevent having your child "remember" his homework just as you're tucking him into bed.

Routines and rituals can make almost any job easier. For example, you can make a standard shopping list of your regular grocery items, sorted by category. Photocopy a supply of the lists, and always keep one on the refrigerator door. Whenever someone notices that something is needed, they simply check it off on the list. Take this list with you when you shop—you'll find that having a familiar list with the items clearly labeled by category will also help your shopping trip be more efficient.

Create a "gift closet" where you can store wrapping paper, tape, gift tags, cards, and a variety of gifts that you purchase whenever you see a perfect choice for someone, or a great sale. That way, you avoid the last-minute rush when you need a birthday gift.

And remember to *delegate!* Look closely at what you are doing, and determine if someone else is better suited to the task. For instance, make a deal with your husband that whoever is the last to get up in the morning gets to make the bed. Create other simple rules that encourage everyone's daily help: when you're done eating, put your dishes in the dishwasher; put your dirty clothes in the laundry room; and so on. Even a three-year-old can do some simple jobs, like picking up toys, or setting the silverware on the table. There are added bonuses to delegating. Encouraging your children to help around the house builds their self-esteem and expands their abilities. By involving your children in the household chores, you are actually helping build a more successful future for them.

Learn How to Ask for What You Want

Start *asking* for things when you want them! This is especially important for women. It is a very feminine trait to drop hints when we want something, instead of asking outright for help. When I was finishing this book, I was getting down to the deadline, and needed some extra time for work on my writing. I starting dropping hints to my husband, mom, and sister—you know, saying things like, "Boy, my book deadline is coming up, and I still have a lot to do." Well, they weren't picking up on my hints, and I was getting very frustrated and feeling unloved. So I finally realized that the direct approach would be best. I said to my husband on a Sunday morning, "Honey, will you watch the kids for three hours so I can work on my book?" And guess what he said? "Sure, I'd be happy to!" I asked my sister, "Want to trade a few babysitting hours this weekend so I can work on my book?" Guess what she said? "Sure, I'd be happy to!" I asked my mom, "Do you mind if I stay an hour later at work today to work on my book?" Guess what she said? "Sure, no problem!" When you are polite and reasonable, you will find that others will be willing to hear your requests with an open mind. (It sure beats stewing about everyone's lack of responsiveness to your hints!)

Once you have organized your time so that you are more efficient and focused on the correct priorities, you will find that it is possible to have a bit of time for yourself every day. I'm not suggesting hours of self-indulgence. Just 30 minutes curled up with a cup of tea and a good book may be just what you need to energize yourself and keep your spirits up. You're worth it!

Taking Care of Your Mind

It has been said that we live "between our ears." In other words, our perception of life is created by our own mind. Cognitive-behavioral therapists tell us, with some authority, *To change your attitude is to change your life.*

You cannot control the things that happen in your life, but you can control how you think about them. You can control the *focus* of your thoughts. It is estimated that we say something to ourselves in our head over 50,000 times every day. What are you saying to yourself? Are you a good cheerleader? Or are you a naysayer?

As parents, we tend to put a lot of pressure on ourselves, and to criticize and condemn ourselves whenever we think we are less than perfect. This negative focus causes us much unhappiness. Lighten up! Ask yourself, "Will this matter ten years from now?" Most often the answer is, "Of course not."

Let go of the guilt! A recent study demonstrated that mothers who worked felt guilty about not being home with the children, and mothers who stayed at home with the children felt guilty about not being in the workplace, and mothers who worked part-time and stayed home part-time felt guilty about giving only 50 percent of themselves to each activity! Stop this now! Wherever you are, you are. Focus on the positive aspects of your life situation, and move forward with your head up!

Practice positive "self-talk." This is the phrase therapists use to describe the monologue we keep up in our heads. Most people aren't even aware of the things they say to themselves. But what you say inside your head has a profound effect on your entire outlook, and even on your success. Practicing positive self-talk is one of the most powerful things you can do to change your life for the better.

Write down some positive statements on a small piece of paper, and keep them with you in your purse or pocket. Whenever you feel sad, overwhelmed, or self-critical, take out your statements and read them (aloud, if possible). Think about each statement as you read it. Repeating these affirmations can give you a real inner boost. Here are some sample statements; you can also make up your own. A few of these affirmations are based on concepts presented by Fran and Lou Cox in their wonderful new book, *A Conscious Life: Cultivating the Seven Principles of Authentic Adulthood* (Berkeley, CA: Conari Press, 1996).

I am a good person.

I am capable and confident.

I am loving and lovable.

I take the time to read to my kids every night, and now they love books.

I love my children, and want what's best for them.

I can learn wonderful and valuable things from the mistakes I make.

I can learn from my emotions.

I can treat myself with love and forgiveness.

What my kids do doesn't define who I am.

My identity is safe and sound inside me, no matter what anyone else says or thinks about me.

Taking Care of Your Body

It was about two years ago. It was the end of the day. I was playing baseball with my three kids. After a while, tired, weak, and sore, I sat on the grass to watch them play. And suddenly it hit me, "I feel *old!*" As I looked down, it hit me again, "I look *fat!*" I thought about my busy schedule, and all I had planned for myself and my family, and I said, "How in the world am I going to take care of myself, my family, and my business with an *old, fat, sore, tired body?* Something has got to change, and it's got to change *now!*" I suddenly realized that with all my years of study, I did not really understand my body, nutrition, or health—and I set about to learn.

Food is Fuel

Look—please don't read this section if you're totally happy with your body, and you have a great, healthy relationship to food. Otherwise, bear with me while I digress for a moment from the main subject here—your kids and how you relate to them. How you relate to food, and what kind of shape you're in, actually have a profound impact on your ability to create the kind of homelife you want with your family, and to give your kids the start they need to have happy and successful lives. I'm not talking about anything as profound as the roots of eating disorders here—although your own healthy relationship to food will certainly promote healthy eating habits in your kids. What I'm talking about is much simpler—it's a simple matter of energy.

Food is fuel. Why didn't anybody ever tell me this before? It's *so* simple. It makes so much sense. But through all my years of rabbit food and diet shakes, nobody ever explained to me the value of food as fuel for living! I either starved or I over-ate; my weight yo-yoed along with my energy level and my happiness level. I must thank Dr. Dean Ornish for his book, *Eat More, Weigh Less,* and Susan Powter for her book, *Stop the Insanity,* for finally getting through to me.

Susan says, "Eat!" You must eat to have energy to live—to raise your children, handle your job, support your marriage. The magic key is this: food does not make us unhealthy, food does not make us fat, food does not rob us of our energy. It is our *poor choices* of food that make us unhealthy, make us fat, and rob us of our energy. I have found that when I make the right food choices, I can eat all day long, as much as I want, and actually *weigh less* and have *more energy* than ever before. I cannot believe that I didn't learn what I needed to know until I was in my thirties! But, then again, the diet industry is one of the biggest—Americans spend over 32 *billion* dollars a year on dieting, which tells me that I'm not alone. Many, many people *still* have not learned. We are all looking for that easy answer, that magic pill, that turns us into trim, fit people, and turns chocolate into a health food.

I'd like to share with you some of the commonsense answers I have discovered that lead the way to a fit, healthy lifestyle. I hope I can give you enough hints to motivate you to learn more about your body, and how you can be fit, healthy, and energetic. I know this is not per se a book on health, but when you are healthy, you can be a much better parent. You will have the energy and stamina to keep up with your kids, and enjoy it!

Once I understood the two major aspects of health, it took 30 days for me to feel years younger—I had more energy, I needed less sleep, I was more relaxed, and happier, and—are you ready for this?—I lost pounds and inches. Just 30 days of making a commitment to take better care of myself, and I saw dramatic differences. Try it—what's 30 days? (You may never go back—I know I won't!) There are two major aspects that caused such drastic changes in me. First, I began to understand the true impact of food, not only on my weight, but on my health, my energy level, and my overall attitude about life. And, second, I admitted what an important role the "E" word (exercise) has on my life.

Fat Makes Us Fat

Food does not make us fat. *Fat* makes us fat. When you reduce the amount of fat in your diet, you will be amazed at how much food you can eat while your body is shrinking. Fat is a sneaky, mean substance. Your body doesn't process it—it stores it! So next time you're tempted to eat a big piece of cheesecake, don't bother—just spread it on your hips! That's where it'll end up, anyway. Average Americans eat 35 to 50 percent of their total calories in fat. Average Americans *need* 15 to 20 percent of their total calories from fat.

Your food choices should be focused on these naturally low-fat food groups:

- Pasta

- Grains

- Whole-Grain Bread

- Rice

- Beans

- Vegetables

- Fruit

- Chicken

- Fish

You should avoid these foods:

- Butter and Margarine

- Unsaturated Oils

- All Fried Foods

- Sweets

- Whole-Fat Dairy Products

- Cheese

- Red Meat

Depending on the shape you're in now, and your levels of blood cholesterol, you may also want to avoid egg yolks, nuts, some dairy products, and oils of any kind. Do consult with a doctor and/or a nutritionist before making any radical changes in your diet.

Making the right food choices will not only help you stay fit, it will keep you healthy, fill you with energy, and lift your spirits.

Yes, Calories Count, Too

Since scientists have brought to our attention the fact that, gram for gram, fat contains more than twice as many calories as carbohydrates, lots of people have jumped on the low-fat bandwagon. Using this method for controlling weight, some people do remarkably well, and some fail miserably. Why? Because advertisers have also jumped on the low-fat bandwagon, and have started labeling *everything* low-fat, lower-fat, reduced-fat and nonfat. The problem here is that low-fat cookies, cakes, frozen desserts, snacks, and junk foods still have a lot of calories and little nutritional value. The best way to combat this problem is to start thinking in terms of whole, natural foods. A good technique for changing your eating habits is to stop concentrating on denial, and start focusing on eating *more of the good stuff*.

Eat When You're Hungry—Stop When You're Full

We all started out as children with this natural concept working beautifully. Then we were *robbed!* Our parents started forcing beets into our mouths, even though our body was saying "No!" We were told to eat because it was lunch time, eat because there was still food on our plate, eat because there are starving kids all over the world, eat because *Mommy's* still hungry, eat because we just spent good money on that hamburger, eat because it's a holiday, eat because it's your favorite kind of cake! Then, as we grew older, we added lots of emotional reasons to eat—I'm depressed, I'll have a candy bar. I'm mad at my mother, I'll eat a piece of cake. I'm 30 pounds overweight already, what does it matter? We need to go back to the *natural* process: eat when you're hungry, stop when you're full.

It takes some real time and energy to begin to understand your body's natural feelings about food. You must *focus* every time you put food to your mouth. Ask yourself, "Am I hungry?" Then eat slowly, stop halfway through your meal, have a glass of water, and ask yourself, "Am I full?" If the answer is *Yes*, then pack up the rest of your meal, or even throw it away. (The starving kids aren't going to get *that* food, anyway. And, better in the trash than on your hips!) There are lots of other ways to help keep your food focus healthy. Try asking the waiter in a restaurant to bring you half the dinner, and box up the other half to take home (restaurant portions are scaled to *adult men*, so unless you're an average-sized adult male, don't even tempt yourself to eat it all!). Try eating the healthy food *first*, along with a glass of water, and fill up before scarfing down the high-calorie stuff. Try eating on a smaller plate, so that when your mother's voice in the back of your head says, "Clean your plate!" it will be a much smaller job!

The "E" Word

When my schedule became very busy, the first thing to go was exercise. How could I find the time? Plus—chasing three kids around was exercise enough, wasn't it? No. I have learned that the time I take to exercise comes back to me tenfold in added energy and the need for less sleep. And, heaven knows, when you're raising kids, you need all the help you can get. I started with a very simple plan: I would find 35 minutes every day for some kind of aerobic exercise (staying in motion for the duration). Some days I took a walk, often with two kids in the stroller. Some days I walked up and down the stairs at the office, some days I walked on my treadmill, some days I did a step-aerobic class with Susan Powter on my VCR. Some days my three kids and I danced to Richard Simmons' "Sweatin' to the Oldies." Sometimes I took the kids to the local high school track, and plopped them in the grassy center with some balls and frisbees and toys as I pranced around the track. What really amazed me was the incredible difference I felt in such a short period of time. Why hadn't I done this sooner? Soon I found that movement became more a part of my life. When I took the kids to the park, I no longer spent the whole time on the blanket with a book in my lap. I now ran, chased, and played more. And when I took the kids to the beach, I actually wore a swimsuit, and played in the water with my gang.

I hope these ideas will both encourage and motivate you. I hope I've given you some (low-fat) food for thought! But don't get me wrong: I'm not saying that your goal should be to wind up looking like Cindy Crawford or Tom Hanks. Rather, the point is that healthy eating and exercise can help you be your best self.

Love and Accept Yourself Exactly as You Are

When I look in the mirror and expect to see a 19-year-old airbrushed *Cosmo* cover girl, I can only feel disappointment and dissatisfaction. But when

I look in the mirror and expect to see a 37-year-old mother of three, I can look with love and acceptance. (Sure, I eat right and I exercise, but I'll never jog down the beach in a string bikini—at least not while I have all my marbles intact!) I also need to remember to look deeper than the surface, and see a woman who is a good parent, a loving wife, a successful business owner, and a person of true value and worth.

Self-love and self-acceptance are critically important for your personal well-being. There comes a time in your life when you must look yourself in the eye and say, "I love you just the way you are." That doesn't mean you stop working to improve yourself! You just love yourself every step of the way.

Society makes it tough for us to accept our physical bodies just as they are. After all, the average American woman is 5'4" and weighs 140 pounds, as described in *Your Vital Statistics*, 1986. The average model that stares at us from just about every magazine and TV commercial stands 5'10" and weighs 119 pounds! Even children's movies are affected by this warped perception of what a female looks like. Cinderella, Ariel, Jasmine, Beauty, Pocahontas, and most other popular cartoon heroines have waists so tiny they can use a Band-Aid for a belt, luxurious flowing manes, and faces that would stop traffic. And take a look at Aladdin, the Beast (*after*, not before), John Smith, and all the princes and heroes—chiseled features, glowing white teeth, and not a bit of body fat anywhere to be found! And all those muscles! It's time we understood the difference between fantasy and reality. It's time we came to love and accept ourselves for who we are and what we look like. It's time to get past the hurtful measuring stick—*good-looking, young, and thin*—and realize that what's most important in life can't be judged by appearance. It's time we put a stop to the rise in anorexia, bulimia, and other eating disorders by setting a realistic example, starting with ourselves.

When you look at yourself in the mirror, stand tall. Look not only at your physical reflection, but at all that you are. It's time to say, "I love me!"

Marriage

(Note to single parents: read this section! Although you may not be married now, you may now or will someday have a significant other, or a spouse. The ideas in this chapter are valuable to building a new relationship, or adding sizzle to an existing relationship!)

The Best Thing That Parents Can Do for Their Children Is to Love Each Other

Again, I'm going to make a slight digression here. And you're welcome to skip the rest of this chapter if your marriage is everything you ever hoped it could be. If there's room for improvement, you might want to read what I have to say, because marriage is the foundation upon which your family is structured. If your marriage is strong, like a solid foundation, your whole family will be strong. This is not to say you will never have problems. But you will have the strength to move through those problems and on to better things. When your marriage partnership is solid, the two of you are stronger than either of you on your own.

The rest of this chapter is devoted to changing not your spouse, but the quality of your relationship. And what does this have to do with kid cooperation? Everything. A stable, loving homelife is impossible in the context of an unstable, unloving marriage.

To create or maintain a strong, stable marriage, you will have to take this first critical step: *You must make a commitment to put your marriage first. You must be willing to put time, effort, and thought into your marriage.*

When I made this statement in a class, one woman, Evelyn, spoke up. She was very quiet, but she spoke with determination. Several other women in the room were nodding their heads as she spoke:

"Elizabeth, I hear you, and I know what you say is right. But I have three preschoolers, I work part-time, I do all my own housework, cooking, and laundry. I just don't have any more energy in me to 'work' on my marriage."

I answered, "Evelyn, I understand! I have three children and my own business! Let me ask you one question: would you like to have three preschoolers, work part-time, do all your own housework, cooking, and laundry, and do it all as a single mother? Because if you take care of everything else, and neglect your marriage, that's what could happen.

Suddenly, every mother who had nodded at Evelyn's original comment was looking at me with wide eyes. The thought that their marriage, which was at the very bottom of their priority list, could be in jeopardy, hit them very hard. I noticed that I now had the complete attention of several fathers who earlier had seemed lost in their own thoughts.

Let's take another look at the commitment statement above, "you must make a commitment to put your marriage first. You must be willing to put time, effort, and thought into your marriage." When you make this commitment, your marriage takes on new life and meaning. The wonderful side effect is that you may fall in love with your spouse all over again. In addition, your children will greatly benefit from your strong relationship. Children feel secure and content when they know that Mom and Dad love each other—particularly in today's world, where 50 percent of marriages end in divorce; half of your children's friends have gone, or are going through a divorce; or maybe it's *your* kids who have survived a divorce and are now living in a new family arrangement. Your children need daily proof that their family life is stable and predictable. When you make a commitment to your marriage, your children will feel the difference. No, they won't suffer from neglect!

They'll blossom if your marriage—and their homelife—is thriving in fertile, rich, and healthy soil.

When you first married, your life was colored by your marriage. Your thoughts, your actions, your feelings were all surrounded by your new love. It was easy to put your mate first. But as married life marched forward, and children entered your relationship, the reasons you fell in love may have begun to fade from your memory. The energy you put into your marriage may have begun to lessen. When couples become parents, it is natural and normal for the focus to change from "the two of us" to "all of us." However, when the "all of us" *overtakes* "the two of us" on a regular basis, your marriage will suffer. So, for the sake of your children, your marriage, and yourself, take the first step to adding sizzle to your relationship, and make that commitment!

Pam tentatively raised her hand. "Okay. I'm willing to make a commitment. But I don't think my husband will. I can't even get him to come to these classes. How can I do it alone? Isn't marriage a two-way street?"

The real beauty of this plan is that whenever one person in a relationship begins to change, it sets off a chain reaction. When you begin to put into practice the methods we are going to discuss, your mate will not be able to stop himself (or herself) from changing. Your mate may not even be conscious of what's happening, but happen it will. When you see the positive changes, you'll be inspired to continue—and your mate will respond in even more positive ways—which will inspire you to continue; and, before you know it, you'll be on your second honeymoon.

Commit to following the suggestions in this book for just two months. At the end of that time, take a look at your marriage. I'll be very surprised if you aren't happy with what you see!

Look for the Good, and Overlook the Bad

You married this person for many good reasons. Your partner has many wonderful qualities. Your first step in adding sizzle to your marriage is to look for the good, and overlook the bad. It is a known fact that when you look for the negative, soon it will be *all* that you see. Do you know people with this kind of outlook? When it's raining, they complain about the rain; when it's sunny, they complain about the dry, brown grass. When they are hungry, they complain about their hunger; and when they are full, they complain that they are stuffed. When the kids are little, they wish they were older; and when they are older, they wish they were young again.

A negative focus can also affect how you see your spouse. You can change "what's in the eye of the beholder" with a simple commitment to look for the good. If you focus on improving your mate, it will only lead to dissatisfaction and anger. If you focus on changing your *view* of your mate, it will lead to a happier marriage, and a happier you. My very favorite quote in the whole world is by William Shakespeare: *There is nothing either good or bad, only thinking makes it so.*

Let's take a look at how your point of view can affect your life:

Negative View	Positive View
He's late again. Dinner's cold. He doesn't care about me. This makes me so mad!	*He's working late again because he's trying to support our family. I appreciate his efforts.*
How you feel: Angry, neglected, used	How you feel: Loved, secure
She spends too much time with the baby—I feel so neglected.	*I'm glad I picked such a dedicated woman to be the mother of my children.*
How you feel: Resentful, guilty	How you feel: Lucky, satisfied
How can he sit there and watch TV while I clean the kitchen? It's not fair. I made dinner, I was with the kids all evening. He never does his share.	*It was really helpful that he picked the kids up from school. And I know I can count on him to take the trash out—he always does it, and I never have to think about it. It's nice to see him sitting with the kids. They sure love their dad.*
How you feel: Resentful, frustrated	How you feel: Contented, secure
I wish she wouldn't nag me about my weight. It doesn't help at all. And she's not so skinny herself anymore! If I want to eat this snack, I will.	*I'm glad she loves me so much that she wants to see me healthy. I'm glad she cares about my appearance.*
How you feel: Defensive, guilty	How you feel: Loved, nurtured

Of course, these are oversimplifications. Emotions are rarely so uncontaminated—there will be lurking resentments and disappointments, defensiveness and anger. You're not going to suddenly transform into Pollyanna, nor should you want to. Couples in a good marriage have the security and skills to deal with their negative emotions as well as their positive ones. Conflicts are as inevitable between a husband and wife as they are between siblings. But do you see the difference that a positive, rather than a negative, outlook can make? You can find something good in every situation. It's a matter of focus. You can also use this principle in rewriting your own inner dialogue. Often it's only our negative self-talk that holds us back from being really happy.

Decide here and now that whenever you catch yourself thinking a negative thought, you will force yourself to change your focus and find something good to think about! It almost seems as if it comes naturally to people in our culture to think negatively. It takes an effort of will to switch to a more positive mode. But it is so worth it! It takes practice and persistence (and it may take therapy—don't discount this as an option); but once you get in the habit, you'll realize the extent to which your thoughts affect your outlook and general sense of well-being.

Give Two Compliments Every Day

Now that you've committed to seeing the good in your mate, it's time to *say it.* This is a golden key to your mate's heart. Our world is so full of negative input, and we so rarely get compliments from other people. When we do get a compliment, it not only makes us feel great about ourselves, it actually makes us feel great about the person giving the compliment! Think about it! When your mate says: "You are such a wonderful human being. I think I married an angel," it not only makes you feel loved, it makes you feel more loving. My husband calls me his angel, and every time he does, I love him more. We have been together for 13 years, and we are still on our honeymoon. One of the reasons is that we both compliment each other—often.

Compliments are easy to give. Compliments are free. Compliments are powerful. You just have to make the effort to do it. Big compliments are major marriage-builders; but, you know what? Little compliments are marriage-builders, too. Whether you compliment your mate on the beautiful job she did painting the house, her pretty new haircut, or the tasty tuna sandwich she made, it *all* counts!

The best compliments are specific. Verbalize your thoughts—don't assume that your spouse simply "knows" how grateful you are, and how appreciative. Your spouse is not a mind reader. "Dinner was good" is better than nothing. But you double the impact of your statement by expanding on your thoughts. Give some detail: "I really enjoyed dinner. The pasta had such a nice spicy flavor, and the chicken was really moist and tender." Instead of "Thanks," try this: "Thanks for picking up the dry cleaning. It sure saved me some valuable time today." Instead of "You look nice," try: "You look so handsome in that sweater—the color matches your blue eyes." Specific compliments tell your partner, "I notice what's special about you. I really appreciate who you are."

Some compliments don't even need to be directly related to anything. You can just walk up to your spouse and murmur, "I'm so glad I married you," or "You're my best friend," or "I thought about you today, and it made me feel happy." How could you not feel great about someone who says such beautiful things to you?

Especially if you're a man, giving compliments may not be your style. Maybe you've always been the strong, silent type. Or maybe you resist the idea of giving this kind of verbal support, because your spouse has been nagging you for it for the past several years, and it's become an issue involving the balance of power between you. If you can, let go of whatever baggage you're carrying on the issue. You won't lose any power in your relationship if you give compliments (or flowers!)—you'll actually gain it. Your spouse may be putty in your hands. Your spouse will look at you in a whole new way.

This is a complex issue for many couples. You might want to look at some of the excellent books that deal with couples skills (I've listed some of my favorites at the end of this chapter); and you may want to consider a few sessions of couples work with a competent marriage counselor, depending on your individual situation.

A wonderful idea is to put at least one compliment a week in writing. A small love note left near your mate's bathroom sink will add love and sparkle for the whole day. Leaving a note in an unexpected place is fun, and adds a light, loving feeling to your day. Try putting a note on the steering wheel of your mate's car, inside a lunch bag, tucked in a book, or in the refrigerator!

Compliments are gifts of love. Dr. Len Fellez said in *Your Child's Self-Esteem*, "There are no small gifts of love. All gifts of love are boundless, absolute and with no limits."

Make this your goal: I will give my mate two compliments every day.

The 60-Second Cuddle

Most people who are dating, and most newlyweds, touch each other all the time. You can almost tell how long a couple has been together by how much they touch. Watch people in a restaurant. The new couple is sitting on the same side of the booth, hip to hip, their hands are entwined, and, if you look under the booth, they're playing footsies! They look into each other's eyes, and you can almost *feel* the love between them. The old married couples sit across from each other, barely touching, and if they accidentally do touch, they say, "Excuse me." They pay more attention to their dinner than to each other.

Touch is critical for healthy human development. New babies who are not touched and cuddled will die. Adults who aren't touched will not physically die, but a certain part of their emotional health will wither away. Virginia Satir, in the book *Chicken Soup for the Soul*, by Jack Canfield and Mark Victor Hansen, says that we need four hugs a day for survival, eight hugs a day for maintenance, and twelve hugs a day for growth.

It *is* possible to bring more romance into your relationship. The first step is to touch each other more often. A wonderful and easy way to approach this idea is to give each other a 60-second cuddle whenever you have been apart. When you first awaken, when you arrive home from work, and any other time that you have been apart: make it a rule that you will take just 60 seconds to cuddle, touch, and connect. Touching and hugging can be addictive. Soon you will find yourselves touching each other more often; and touch leads to romance in many other ways.

If you have a partner who would not be willing to make this commitment, that's okay. It only takes one of you to put this plan into action. Your unsuspecting mate will be going along with it—just because it feels so good.

Here's another idea for adding more physical love to your relationship. Whenever your partner gives you a hug, let *your partner* end it! You'll get a very loving feeling when the cuddle lasts longer.

Make this promise to yourself: whenever we've been apart, we'll come together with a 60-second cuddle.

Use Two Ears and Two Eyes to Listen

Remember the lovebirds in the restaurant? They look into each other's eyes, and really listen to each other. The food on the table is window dressing—it's not at all the focus of their attention. The old married couple, on the other hand, look around the restaurant, eavesdrop on other people's conversations, stare out the window, or read while they're waiting for their food, and look relieved when their dinner arrives. Yet when these two people first met, they probably stayed up half the night just talking! When a relationship is new, a couple doesn't worry about who gets to talk more, or what they talk about. They just feel good being together, and talking happens naturally. Each is riveted by what the other is saying.

Part of the process of falling in love is sharing thoughts, ideas, events from the past, and dreams. Part of the reason we fall in love with someone is because that person *really* listens to us, and, in doing so, makes us feel special and loved. A wonderful way to add sparkle to your relationship is to become a better listener. This is so easy! Just look at your partner's face, and really listen. Don't interrupt, don't plan what you are going to say next, don't spend time looking around. Just listen. A wonderful side effect to this plan is that your mate will begin talking to you more, and listening to you more.

Make this promise to yourself: when my partner talks, I will look into his/her eyes and really listen.

Every Week: Time for Two

It is very difficult for your marriage to thrive if you spend all your time being Mom and Dad. You must also spend time together on a regular basis as husband and wife. Life can get so busy raising children, and working to support your family, that you and your spouse probably rarely connect in a way that would nurture the love between you. It can be impossible to nurture your love relationship when you always have a baby on your hip, a toddler at your knee, or an older child participating in every conversation. We've all seen a version of the cartoon that shows two older people staring at each other across the table and asking, "Who are you?" after all the children have left the home. The long-term benefit of connecting with your spouse is obvious. The short-term benefits are not so obvious, but are just as critical. When you nurture your marriage, everything about your life will flow more easily. When you feel secure in your marriage, you will be a better parent, a better worker, a better person!

The best way to nurture your marriage is to schedule time *every week* for just the two of you. My husband and I have a standing date every single Friday night. We have had our date-night since our first child was born. It doesn't always mean we get a sitter, dress up, and paint the town red. Sometimes we just go for a walk, or have a picnic. Sometimes we grab a sandwich, and sit by the water and talk. When we had a newborn in the house, our night out was reduced to two hours; or we took the newborn along in a carry-pouch. Now if a baby-sitter isn't available, we work a trade with my sister or a friend. If we have to stay home, we set the kids up with a snack and a movie, and we snuggle on the sofa and enjoy our quiet time together. The key is that we both know that Friday night is *our* night. As busy as we both are, this special time has been critical to keeping our love and our marriage strong.

Make this promise to yourself: we will plan time every week for just the two of us.

Communicate With Love

Every relationship has problems. People are different. Their thoughts are different, their needs are different. Problems are normal. It is how we deal with those problems that can make or break our marriage. Couples can get so focused on their problems, that everything good in the marriage is eclipsed. That's when divorce happens. Each member of the couple eventually gets into a new relationship, and—surprise—it has problems, too!

I heard this story many years ago, and have often thought how powerfully it demonstrates human nature:

One day, a gatekeeper to a city was approached by a visitor. The visitor asked, "What manner of people live in your city?" The gatekeeper asked the visitor, "What manner of people lived in your last city?" To which the visitor replied, "Terrible people! They were rude and nosy and unkind. It was hard to find a friend. The city was full of sadness and anger." "Alas," the gatekeeper replied, "You will find the same manner of people here." A few days later, a second visitor arrived at the gate.

He, too, asked the gatekeeper, "What manner of people live in your city?" To which the gatekeeper replied, "What manner of people lived in your last city?" The visitor answered, "Good people. They were kind and thoughtful. I had many friends. The city was full of happiness and love." "Welcome!" said the gatekeeper. "You will find the same manner of people here."

Remember—your thoughts control your outlook on life, and the choices you make about what kind of life to live. When you approach your world with love and kindness, you will tend to find it returned. This is ever so true in marriage. Whenever you communicate with your mate, try to understand how the other person feels on the receiving end of your communication. Try to phrase your words so that your mate will be eager to help you, not anxious to block you out! Pretend you are on the receiving end of these statements, and see how different they feel:

Why don't you ever call me when you're going to be late? You're inconsiderate.	*I'd really appreciate it if you called when you're going to be late.*
You always yell at Jimmy like that. It's no wonder he won't listen to you.	*I think Jimmy might respond better if you used a calmer tone of voice.*
Don't you know where the hamper is? Sometimes I think I have four *kids in this house!*	*I'd like it if you could put your socks in the hamper.*

It will help your relationship if you avoid making "blaming" statements: "You never ...," "You always ...," "You are such a ...," "You make me ...." When you approach your spouse about a problem, phrase your words as an "I" statement: "I would like it if ...," "I feel happy when ...," "I think that ...." Phrasing things this way avoids making your spouse feel defensive, and opens up the doors for listening.

I strongly recommend that you take the time to learn how to better understand your spouse. There are many good books, classes, video programs, and counselors that can help you keep your marriage strong and healthy. Two books that I recommend are *Couple Skills* by Matthew McKay, Ph.D., Patrick Fanning, and Kim Paleg, Ph.D., and *Men Are From Mars, Women Are From Venus* by Dr. John Gray. Take the time to read them—your marriage is worth it!

Promise yourself: I will communicate with love.

Further Reading and References

Cox, Fran and Lou *A Conscious Life: Cultivating the Seven Principles of Authentic Adulthood* (Berkeley, CA: Conari Press, 1996)

Ornish, Dean *Eat More, Weigh Less* (New York, HarperCollins, 1993)

Powter, Susan *Stop the Insanity!* (New York, Simon & Schuster, 1993)

Brandreth, Gyles Daubeney *Your Vital Statistics* (New Jersey, Citadel Press, 1986)

Fellez, Len *Your Child's Self-Esteem* (Seattle, WA, Kids Unlimited, 1990)

McKay, Matthew; Fanning, Patrick; and Paleg, Kim *Couple Skills* (Oakland, CA, New Harbinger Publications, 1994)

Gray, John *Men Are From Mars, Women Are From Venus* (New York, Harper-Collins, 1992)

Reminder Page— How Can You Take Care of Everyone Else if You Don't Take Care of Yourself?

Take Care of Yourself

- Relax your standards, get organized

- Say no when you need to

- Create routines to simplify your life

- Ask for what you want

- Maintain a positive attitude

- Eat right and exercise

- Love and accept yourself exactly as you are

- Take a bit of time every day for yourself

Take Care of Your Marriage

Make a commitment to:

- Put time, effort, and thought into your marriage

- Look for the good, overlook the bad

- Give two compliments every day

- Greet each other with a 60-second cuddle

- Listen with two eyes and two ears

- Every week, make time for two

- Communicate with love

9

Ideas—Not Answers

Parents often ask me specific questions about their children. After they ask, they literally hold their breath, open their eyes wide, and listen carefully—as if the *one right answer* were about to be announced! Let me tell you this—there are *many* right solutions to any parenting problem, just as there are many good choices from a menu at a restaurant, or many routes to the same destination. You can ask the same question of five parenting experts, and receive five totally different answers. You can find an expert to validate almost any child-rearing method. You can find experts who will completely contradict one another, even as they each present a sound and reasonable explanation for their opinion.

The key to handling any problem in parenting, or finding the right solution to any problem, lies in having a plan, a method, a goal, and a purpose. Parents who think *in advance* about their parenting methods, and have a plan for dealing with the daily adventures of raising their children, will have a much easier time than those who "shoot from the hip." Parents who understand the typical behaviors of children, and who have specific skills and methods at their disposal, can weather almost any storm.

In this section I will give you sound, reasonable answers to common questions. Sometimes I'll give you two answers! Some of the pairs of answers will sound as if they come from two different books, or even two different worlds. The reason for having such different answers lies in the differences that exist in families. Every family is different, every child is different, and every situation is different. It is presumptuous of any parenting professional to think that he or she can provide exact answers to any family question without knowing all the details of the particular family, the personalities of the people involved, and what methods have been unsuccessfully tried. When raising a child, nothing is black and white. What works for one family will not work for another. What works for one child will not work for his sibling. And it's even true that what works for one child *today* will not work for that same child *tomorrow*. What I hope to give you are *ideas*. You can review the options, and choose the one that seems to best fit your needs. Sometimes none of the answers on a particular topic will seem right for you; but the answer I've given should give you enough ideas for you to create your *own* solution. With the knowledge and understanding of different viewpoints, you can make sound parenting decisions that are right for *you*.

Q: I have tried to use time out with my three-year-old, Tyler, whenever he hits his little sister. The *idea* is to put him in the bathroom for three minutes. The *reality* is that I have to drag or carry him to the bathroom, and then he just follows me out. We end up with a 20-minute battle, which ends with me holding the door closed, and Tyler kicking the door and screaming. I'm sure this isn't teaching him anything—and it just makes me furious! What should I do?

A: You're right! When you try to put a strong-willed child in time out, the ensuing battle undermines any lesson you're trying to teach. There is a very effective way to use time out with Tyler, which will teach him a lesson, but avoid the battle. First, you need to remind yourself of the reason why you are using time out: to teach Tyler how to handle his anger at his sister without hitting her. In other words, you are *not* using time out to punish him, but simply to put an immediate stop to his misbehavior. With that goal in mind, you can see that the *length of time* spent in time out is not important. Next time Tyler hits his sister, this is what you can try:

Tyler: (Hits sister)

Parent: (Quickly goes to Tyler, kneels down at his eye level, takes him by the shoulders, and speaks in a very stern voice) Tyler. No hitting. Time out. (Parent takes Tyler into the bathroom.) "You may come out when you can play without hitting."

Tyler:	(Immediately comes out of bathroom and hits his sister again)
Parent:	You are not ready to come out yet. Time out. You may come out when you can play without hitting.
Tyler:	(Comes out of bathroom) "I'm ready now." (He plays nicely with his sister for 20 minutes. When he hits her again, parent repeats the above scene. The next day Tyler doesn't hit quite so much, and the parent follows the same procedure each time hitting occurs. Within a week, Tyler's hitting has been brought under control.)

The beauty of this technique is that the parent is giving the child a very clear message of trust and love. The parent is helping the child to understand that he can control his own actions, and the consequences of his actions. He is capable of deciding when his time out is over, and he is capable of playing without hitting. In this way, the parent can avoid the 20-minute battle of *making* the child stay in time out.

When we used this method on two-year-old David, he would often say, "I'm done," *as we were walking him to the bathroom!* In that case, I would not punish him by continuing to put him in time out, because if he *really was* done with the misbehavior, then I had already achieved my goal—helping David to behave appropriately.

Another option you have is to avoid using time out in favor of other methods of discipline you are learning in this book. There are some methods that will work wonders with some children, but totally fail with others. Only you know your child well enough to determine which methods are effective for you.

> **Q: I've read several articles that address the issue of spanking. Often, the writer says it's okay to spank if the child is in danger—for instance, if a toddler is running into the street, or reaching out to touch a hot burner on the stove. Are these times when a few pops on the rear end are okay?**

A: I've read this too, and I must admit it baffles me. Why in the world would we want to teach our children about safety by hurting them? Does your ski instructor jab you with his ski pole to teach you not to jump off the chairlift? A parent who believes that a spanking is the only effective way to teach a young child about safety issues is not giving the child enough credit. Children—even little ones—can indeed learn about safety through our teaching them. As a matter of fact, through teaching they will learn much more, as they can absorb the *reason* for the rule, and, over time, can learn to make good decisions on their own.

I watched two friends one summer teach their toddlers not to run in the street. Mom "A" gave her toddler a swat on the rear every time he went in the street. Mom "B" picked up her toddler, looked him in the eye, and said, "No street. Dangerous. Stay by Mommy." By the end of the summer, both children learned to stay out of the street. Which child understood *why?* And which child has better communication with his mother?

Q: Tan, my 14-year-old son, has a smart mouth. When I ask him to do something, he'll often look me in the eye, put his hands on his hips, and mimic my request in an irritating singsong voice. What ensues is usually a full-scale battle over a tiny issue. Now I understand why *my* father used to threaten to "slap that silly grin off your face!" But what do I do to control this behavior?

A: Congratulations! You have a typical, healthy adolescent worth keeping. The behavior you've described perfectly demonstrates an adolescent's struggle to become his own person. Tan is expressing his desire to be an adult in charge of his own life, while acknowledging that he is still a kid and must do what you say. You mentioned that your own father had to deal with this behavior from you, and I'm sure his father had the same problem, and I'm sure *his* father had the same problem, and, well, you get the picture! Now that you know that the behavior is normal, you can decide on a method of action that will not *empower* the behavior. I suggest that you try this technique:

Father: Tan, you can go out *after* your chores are done.

Tan: (Mimicking) Oh? I can go out *after* my chores are done?

Father: That's correct. Thank you. (And he walks away)

What Father has just done is give a clear message to his son that his request must be obeyed, and that he'll not be sucked into an argument over the issue. By adding a "thank you," he implies that Tan will do as asked with no further discussion. If Tan does not obey, then Father can apply a logical consequence that he feels is appropriate.

If you are not comfortable with this idea, you can try a different plan of attack. Next time your child uses an inappropriate tone of voice with you, look him straight in the eye and say, "I will not listen when you talk to me that way." Then turn, and calmly leave the room. Often, being left standing alone will give your child a very powerful message that his behavior is unacceptable.

What you *don't* want to do is overreact and call great attention to this behavior through shouting or punishing. This will typically only make the behavior worse. What you *can* do is make use of a quiet, peaceful moment between you to express your feelings about the behavior in a nonthreatening way. This is more apt to gain your child's cooperation than anything else.

Q: I have four-year-old twins, Amy and Alex, and a two-year-old, Amanda. My biggest problem is getting out the door in the morning. We have to leave by 8:00 to get the kids to daycare and me to work on time. The twins are forever dawdling, Amanda's usually fussing, and I'm usually angry and late by the time we leave. How can I solve this problem?

A: Boy, do I understand! When my kids were one, three, and five, I had the same problem. In a few more years, your kids will be able to share some of the responsibility for the morning routine; but, for now, it's all up to you. I suggest a plan of attack. Once you superorganize your plan, you *can* get out the door on time, and even have a smile on your face.

First, take a look at your schedule, and decide if there are any changes that can be made to relieve some of your pressure. Could you and your spouse share responsibility in a way that makes the morning run more smoothly? Would getting up 30 minutes earlier make a difference? Is the daycare your children are in the best choice, or is there a closer location, with more flexible hours that might be a better choice? Is it possible in your workplace to start work 30 minutes later, and leave 30 minutes later?

Create a detailed morning and evening schedule for yourself, including a checklist. Making sure that everything gets done in a timely manner will help keep your mornings organized, and will help you leave on time (and in a good mood) every day.

Do as many tasks as you can *the night before*. For example, when you are done cleaning up the dinner dishes, set the table for breakfast. Put out the bowls, spoons, napkins, and cereal. Put the milk in a small container on the bottom shelf of the refrigerator. Presto! When the older kids get up, they can serve themselves breakfast.

Make it a part of your evening routine to lay out your children's clothes for the next day. Collect coats, shoes, hats, and backpacks, and place them by the door so that you don't have to scramble in the morning to find everything.

Getting the kids dressed is usually the biggest problem. Sometimes when you have a big problem, the best way to handle it is to—get rid of it!

This idea involves starting out the night before. After your children have their bath, *don't* put cute little footie pajamas on them! Put on tomorrow's clothes. Honest! Most children's clothing can be slept in all night without a wrinkle. (If your little one still sleeps in disposable diapers, you can put underwear over the diaper, in the morning, pull the diaper off, wipe the bottom, and you're ready for the day!) Trust me, this idea alone will save you about 15 minutes per child—with three, that's an extra 45 minutes! I can hear some of you laughing right now, but it's time we figured out that we can't be super-human and do everything perfectly. Sure, your mother will probably have a heart attack when she hears what you're up to, but I bet she didn't have the same time demands and pressure in her day that you do. Ideas like these can save you work time, so that you can have more playtime with your children— and what's more important, anyway?

> **Q: I have two children, Mark, age eight, and Heather, age ten. My biggest problem is getting out the door in the morning. We have to leave by 7:30 to get the kids to school and me to work on time. Mark is forever dawdling, Heather's usually primping, and I'm usually finding everyone's lost homework, making lunches, and signing permission slips. Typically I'm angry and we're all late by the time we leave. How can I solve this problem? (Sound familiar?)**

A: Once children reach first or second grade, depending on their maturity, they need to have the responsibility for handling their own morning routine. Allowing children this responsibility is a good first step in helping them be- come successful adults. It gives them the practice they need to learn how to take care of themselves. Children this age are very capable of dressing them- selves, serving themselves breakfast, making their own lunches, and gather- ing and organizing all their schoolwork. Good, loving parents who always take over these chores for their children are not doing them any favor. In fact, they are robbing their children of the grand opportunity to learn how to get along in the world on their own. Now, this doesn't mean that you should tell your children, "Tomorrow you are on your own. The bus leaves at 8:00—with or without you!" Children need guidelines, assistance, and practice to create and adhere to a routine that works for them. They also need to know that this isn't a game, and that you are counting on them to uphold their part of the routine.

A great method for jump-starting your new morning plan is to use what I call "Morning Magic." This is simply a piece of paper that lists your children's morning responsibilities (along with a picture for children just beginning to read—you can even draw your own stick people). Your children can help you prepare the list, and they can post several copies where they can see them in the morning. Add a few time gauges so that your children know if they're dawdling or running on time. Keep the schedule simple. It may look like this:

Morning Magic

7:00	1. Get up.
	2. Eat breakfast.
	3. Get dressed, brush hair and teeth.
7:30	4. Make lunch.
	5. Feed the dog.
	6. Collect books and homework.
8:00	7. Put shoes, coat, lunch, and backpack by the door.

I have found that the list alone is enough to organize most children in a way that allows them to take control of their morning. A *few* gentle reminders along the way—"How are you doing on your Morning List?"—typically keep a child on target.

There is always the child, however, who can conveniently ignore any number of lists or charts, and insist on making the morning routine *your* problem. Don't let this happen! If you have one of these kids, you may need to go one step farther. You may need to add a consequence for failure to be ready on time. *Your* chart may look like the one on page 162.

Remember to try a simple chart *without consequences* first, as this gives your children a reasonable chance to get themselves organized. Only add the consequences after you have given the chart a fair try, and your children are still late and dawdling.

Q: HELP! Bedtime around our house is a disaster! Xavier, our four-year-old, refuses to go to sleep! "One more drink." "I have to go potty." "I'm scared." "I'm not tired." After an hour of this, I usually end up screaming at him, he cries himself to sleep, then I feel so guilty, my whole night is ruined.

A: If it is any consolation, the "bedtime is a disaster" problem comes up in almost every class and lecture I give. It is a universal problem. Let's examine it in five parts:

- Why Do Kids Fight Sleep?

- How Do Parents Make the Problem Worse?

- Solution: Idea Number 1

- Solution: Idea Number 2

- Solution: Idea Number 3

Why Do Kids Fight Sleep?

From an adult perspective, sleep is a precious commodity. Usually we don't feel as if we get enough sleep, which is our time to air out our brain,

---

Morning Magic

This list must be completed by 8:00* sharp:

7:00	1. Get up.
	2. Eat breakfast.
	3. Get dressed, brush hair and teeth.
7:30	4. Make lunch.
	5. Feed the dog.
	6. Collect books and homework.
8:00	7. Put shoes, coat, lunch and backpack by the door.

You are responsible for completing this list. There will be no reminders. If all items on this list are not completed correctly by the time listed, the following consequence will occur that day (no discussion or second chances):

1. Immediately after school: make tomorrow's lunch, lay out clothes for tomorrow, organize backpack.

2. Bedtime will be one hour earlier so you are more refreshed and able to follow the chart tomorrow.

---

* This time should be 10–15 minutes before departure to allow inspection and whatever time you might need to help complete tasks if they are not done.

refresh our body, and enjoy the physical sensation of a cozy bed. But to kids sleep is purely and simply an unwanted interruption in a life full of fun. For some reason, kids never acknowledge the feeling of "tiredness" as meaning "I need sleep." What's more, for many children, sleep represents an unwanted separation from the important people in their lives. Being in bed is too lonely, too boring, and no fun at all!

How Do Parents Make the Problem Worse?

I hear so many parents complain that they can't get their children to go to sleep. Let's take a close look at this concept. We cannot make a child go to *sleep,* but we can make him go to *bed.* There's a big difference between the two. If you even try to control a child's ability to fall asleep, you are losing the battle before you begin. (The only exception is a nursing mother, with a sleepy baby!) Even our children themselves cannot really control when they *go to sleep.* The most we as parents can do is to make the environment conducive to sleep; sleep will then come on its own.

Parents tend to make matters even worse by their own ambivalence about bedtime rules. When a child asks for "one more kiss," or "one more drink," he usually gets it. When he asks to go potty, he gets help. When he continues to get out of bed, he gets conversation (maybe not great conversation, but contact nonetheless).

It's time that you decide what your own feelings are about bedtime. It's time that you analyze your feelings and needs, and your child's feelings and needs, and determine exactly how you will handle bedtime. I'm going to give you three ideas for solutions. You may feel very good about one, or you may wish to combine some of the points from each one. The most important guideline is that you *decide what you are going to do, and then stick with it.* Parents usually create their own problems by dancing around and between all the different bedtime methods until they get themselves angry and their kids confused. So, the first step is to decide exactly how you will handle bedtime. The second step is to communicate your rules to your child. The third step is to implement the plan.

Solution: Idea Number 1

It's time to have a talk with Xavier! Sit down with him some time during the day (not an hour before bedtime!), and set the rules. Your words might sound something like this: "Xavier, bedtime has been a pretty yucky time around here lately. I usually end up yelling at you, and you end up crying by the end of the night. We aren't going to do this anymore. We now have a new plan. I have made you a new *Bedtime Chart* and here it is," (page 164).

Xavier's Bedtime Chart

1. Put on pajamas.

2. Have a snack.

3. Brush teeth.

4. Read 5 books. [Or read for 15 minutes.]

5. Get drink of water. Go potty.

6. Turn on night-light.

7. Mommy/Daddy goes downstairs.

8. Xavier lies quietly in bed and goes to sleep.

Your chart is a large piece of poster board with neatly displayed steps, illustrated, if your child can't yet read—stick people will do!

Post the chart on Xavier's bedroom door, at his eye level. Have him help you follow the chart each night by asking him, "What's next?"; and then give him praise for following each step. For many children, the chart alone provides the consistency and routine that will help them cooperate with you at bedtime. Will Xavier stay in bed on the first night when you reach step number 8? Of course not! How you react to his escape will make or break your new routine. If you give him his kiss, or his drink, or help him go potty, you will be telling him that nothing has changed, and he will continue his bedtime games ad infinitum. There are several ways to handle this:

Option 1: When Xavier shows up downstairs or at the kitchen door, take him by the hand and walk him, or carry him, back to bed. Do not engage him in conversation beyond one simple sentence: "The chart says it's time for you to stay in bed." Ignore his pleas for drinks, kisses, or buttered toast. Don't answer his questions about what time it is, what day is tomorrow, or how long until Christmas. After you put him back in bed, stay by the door. The minute he walks out, turn him around and repeat the process. Be prepared! The first night, Xavier will be furious. He may cry, scream, or bang on his door. Just hold your breath, and repeat after me: "This too shall pass." Trust me, by morning, he will have his mind on other, more pleasant things. The next night, the same ritual. And the next. And the next. Eventually, Xavier will give up and stay in bed. Depending on the child, this may take two nights, or it could take twenty! But as long as you stay calm, and outlast him, you *will* win! And then forever and ever, bedtime will be a peaceful, calm time, and you can reclaim your evenings.

Option 2: If you know your child will continue to escape after step 8, then add step 9:

> 9. Xavier will have two "Get-Out-of-the-Bedroom-Free" cards. He may come out for potty, water, kisses, or hugs—two times only. [He must give you his ticket when he comes out.]

If he comes out after the two times, you will need to impose an appropriate consequence. Let him know in advance what this will be, and then stick to it. It may be that he will not be given his "escape" cards the next night or that you will hold the door closed so that he cannot come out (if you do this, make sure you leave his night-light on, and reassure him that you are on the other side of the door); or you can use another related consequence. Be firm!

Solution: Idea Number 2

Personally, I always wonder why parents insist on making bedtime such a battleground. Every night, night after night, it's hours of nagging, yelling, crying, and frustration. I prefer to create a loving, peaceful routine to end our day. I prefer to take advantage of the bedtime hour to bond with my children through a loving ritual.

You can take the pressure off yourself by revising your expectations. If you envision Xavier waltzing up the stairs, calling goodnight over his shoulder, and tucking himself into bed with a smile on his face, you will be sorely disappointed. Rather, look at bedtime as a wonderful opportunity for that quality time with your kids that we all talk about, but don't seem to get much of. Develop a bedtime routine that includes special quiet time for you and your child. Include a cuddle or a back rub. Read together. Talk together. Stay with him until he's ready to settle down for the night, or even until he's asleep. I've talked with many parents who follow this pattern, and they say their children fall asleep quickly, knowing that they can count on someone being there for them.

Me? I lead a very busy life. My days are full of teaching, writing, and running my business. I cherish every moment with my three children. I have two special times that are reserved especially for my family. Weekends. And bedtime. On nights when I'm home, we have a very special, loving bedtime routine. We all put our pajamas on together, brush our teeth together, then we snuggle together in the kids' king-size bed (they usually all sleep together, their choice), and I read to them. I'll read for 30 minutes to an hour, until I begin to read myself to sleep! Then we turn out the light, and pile up like a Mama cat and her kittens, and cuddle to sleep. Most nights, when my three little angels are asleep, I then get up for some husband-time or me-time. Other nights, Mama cat falls asleep right along with her kittens. I think it's a lovely, peaceful, wonderful way to end our day.

Solution: Idea Number 3

When your children are of an age when they can read books independently, you can initiate a very effective bedtime method. The method is based on the fact I stated earlier: you cannot make a child go to sleep, but you can make a child stay in bed. This idea also has its foundation in the concept of letting children learn important life lessons through natural consequences. Here goes:

Parent: Son, I've been thinking that it's time you take responsibility for your own sleep-time. You are now capable of making this kind of decision. This is what we're going to do. Nine o'clock will be your bedtime—this means I expect you to be in your bed by nine. You may choose to read for a while before you go to sleep. You can decide when to turn your light out. Just keep in mind that we get up at 6:30 AM, and it's hard to get up if you don't get enough sleep.

One word of warning! Many children will get so excited about being able to stay up as long as they want—that they will! The first night you may see the reading light still on at 11:30 PM. That's okay. The next day will be a great learning experience: your children will learn what it feels like to function on too little sleep. (We all know what that feels like!) The key to success here is to refrain from lecturing. Just put your arm around your child, and express your sympathy about having to live through the day feeling so tired. Trust me! The next night that light will be out much, much earlier!

Which Option Is the Right One?

You now have a variety of new ideas for handling bedtime. I have worked with parents who have found great success through any one of these options, or through variations of their own. Follow your heart. The right answer is different for every family. And whichever method you choose will be the right one for you. Please remember that no matter what method you choose, you will not cause lifelong emotional or psychological problems for your child! Children are far more resilient than that. A child's life is made up of many little pieces, somewhat like a jigsaw puzzle; how you handle bedtime is just one little piece of the puzzle. You have to look at the whole picture, at every aspect of the child's life, to see how the pieces all come together to create and form who that child is.

Many, many parents ask me how to solve their bedtime problems with their children from toddler age to about eight years old. I almost never hear about a bedtime issue with children from age nine and up. I think bedtime is kind of like the problem of putting shoes on the wrong feet—we fuss over it when they are young, but it ceases to be an issue by the time they hit elementary school.

Now is the time for you to review all the bedtime suggestions, decide upon your new bedtime routine, and follow through. It will take time to switch from the current bedtime chaos to your new method so be patient, be persistent, and sweet dreams!

Q: My three-year-old, Stephanie, has a very difficult time sharing. She's possessive about not only her things, but everything! My sister's three-year-old shares beautifully. When they are together, I get so embarrassed over Stephanie's temper tantrums. What's the best way to encourage my daughter to share?

A:

The Toddler's Creed

What's mine is mine, that's plain to see,
And what looks like mine must surely be,
If I like it a lot I'll lay my claim,
(If I might like it someday, that's kind of the same),
If you want it now, then I must too,
But change your mind, and I'll change my view,
If it's in my room, if it's in my hand,
If it's in my house, don't you understand?
It might be important to play with someday,
But what will happen if I give it away?

From a young child's egocentric point of view, there is only one way to label possessions—"mine." Sharing does not fit well within this definition. It will help you, however, if you begin to look at learning to share in the same way in which you look at learning to read. Both are developmental issues—a child does not come into this world reading or sharing; both must be learned.

There is no magical age when a child can suddenly share. Learning to share is influenced by a child's environment: how many siblings she has, as well as their genders and ages; the amount of exposure she has had to children her age, and in what context (a structured preschool versus a free-for-all play group, for instance); and whether she has had any training that would teach her to share. The ability to share is also affected by a child's distinct personality—an intense, strong-willed child will find sharing more difficult than an easygoing child.

There are a number of ways in which you can encourage your child to share. First, model sharing for her and label it as such. For instance, when you hand her a piece of your cookie, say, "Stephanie, here's a piece of my cookie. I like to share with you. It makes me happy to share." Encourage her to share her toys with you, and give her praise when she does so. This is especially important if your child has no siblings. Also, it's easier for a child to share with her parents than her peers, and this creates a good opportunity for teaching sharing. If you do have more than one child, it's important that you decide what your family rules for sharing are, and make sure that everyone understands them. I strongly suggest that 50 percent of the toys and games you purchase for your children be for "everyone," so that joint ownership is a regular experience. The other half of the toys should be assigned specific owners, so that your child feels she has things she can claim as her own. Never shame or embarrass your child for not sharing. This will only create more negative feelings about it, and more resistance.

Prepare your child in advance for those times when she must share. For example, before another child comes over to visit, you can say, "Stephanie, your cousin Molly is coming over to visit. She's going to be fun to play with! She'll want to play with your toys when she is here. You may choose three of your special things to put away in the hall closet, and the rest of your things you and Molly can play with together." Then, when Molly arrives, spend the first few minutes playing with them to set the pace for the interaction. If Stephanie has an I-don't-want-to-share temper tantrum, you have several options:

1. Take her aside to a quiet room until she calms down. Remind her that Molly is there to play with her and her toys.

2. Offer her a choice: "You can share nicely with Molly, or you can go up to your room for a while and she can play alone until you're ready to share."

3. Distract her with another toy or activity.

4. Use a kitchen timer to allow each child a chance to play with a disputed toy. Usually three to five minutes is an adequate amount of time.

5. Help them work out their own solution through a problem-solving process:

   • State the problem

   • List possible solutions

   • Review the solutions and pick one to use

   • Execute the plan

> **Q: Why is it that my four-year-old always acts up in public? He whines, he fusses, he won't cooperate—he pushes all my buttons. I'm almost afraid to take him anywhere, for fear I'll have to live through another embarrassing episode. Do I just have to wait until he grows out of it?**

A: If you do wait, he won't grow out of it: *it* will grow out of control, and you'll be facing a 12-year-old who still has public tantrums.

There are two reasons why children often exhibit their worst behavior in public places. The first reason is that our expectations are unreasonable.

We take a four-year-old with us out to dinner with friends at 8:00 PM, her usual bedtime, and expect her to sit prettily with her hands in her lap for two hours. We take an active toddler on an airplane, and expect him to eat a bag of peanuts and look out the window at all the pretty clouds. We take children shopping at Toys 'R' Us, and we expect them to keep their hands to themselves and not ask for anything. We take our kids to the mall on a sunny Saturday afternoon, and expect them to follow us around like happy little puppies.

The second reason our kids misbehave in public is—we teach them to! The minute we are out in public with an eager audience, we tend to let the rules that we enforce at home bend, sway, and crack. We avoid disciplining our children in public, and they learn that they can act up and get away with it!

There are a number of ways to get control of public behavior. The first is to have realistic expectations, and be prepared in advance to make the trip run more smoothly. Begin by learning more about appropriate behavior for your child's current age group. It helps to know that most two-year-olds have lie-down-and-scream tantrums when they are tired and hungry. It helps to know that a bored nine-year-old will stir up trouble. When you understand what behavior is normal, you can do your best to ward off the negative behavior by being prepared in advance. As an example, if you are going to be shopping with your child for a long afternoon, make sure you bring along snacks, juice, and a portable toy or activity, like silly putty or a slinky. If you are going out to a restaurant, call ahead to be sure they offer a children's menu and are child-friendly (for instance, do they offer crayons to color with?). When at the restaurant, ask for a particular table that looks child-friendly (a roomy booth, next to the fish tank, close to the bathroom, etc.).

Communicate your expectations *in advance* to your child. Take a few moments in the car before entering the store or restaurant to review appropriate manners. Be specific. "We are going in the store now. I expect you to stay beside me. Walk only, no running. Use a quiet, inside voice. Look with your eyes, do not touch with your hands."

I'm sorry to have to tell you this, but even with the best-laid plans, you will still face public misbehavior. There is one critical key to handling public problems: *stop worrying about strangers' opinions.* I know it's hard, but you can do it. When you begin to focus on your child's behavior instead of on the spectators, you will work from a position of strength. When you focus on your child, you can indeed be firm and use all the wonderful skills you now possess to bring your child's behavior under control.

What if your child is out of control, and you've tried all your skills (make a statement, give a choice, give clear instructions, use Grandma's Rule, make something talk, use humor), but nothing works? That is the time for a "significant training session." You can do any one of a variety of things, but the purpose is to do something that opens your child's eyes wide and makes a major impact. Try one of these:

- Take your child out to the car for a time out. Put him in the car while you sit on the hood, reading a magazine. Tell him, "When you're ready to behave, we'll go back in the store."

- Whisk your child to a private corner, hold him close, and get him to talk about what's bothering him, then clarify your expectations. Sometimes a few moments of peaceful connection is enough to smooth out the situation.

- Leave the cart full of groceries, the restaurant table full of food, or already chosen clothing with a cashier, apologize, pay (in the case of the restaurant), and *go straight home.* (This has the greatest impact if your child typically enjoys a shopping trip, or if the clothing is for him.)

- Finish the outing as quickly as you can. Hire a baby-sitter for the offending child for the *next* shopping trip or restaurant meal. Without anger or criticism say, "Your behavior on our last trip was unacceptable. Today you can stay home."

If you are prepared in advance, have a plan of action handy, and follow your own rules, your child will learn to understand that the same rules that apply at home also apply in public. You child's public tantrums will soon become a thing of the past.

Q: How can I get my 14-year-old daughter to be more respectful to me? This seems like one of the hardest things to enforce. She sasses me, calls me names, and argues with me. I can control her actions—but not her mouth!

A: Disrespect triggers anger and confusion in parents, because it hits us right in the heart. Here's the child we love so much, and take such good care of, treating us so badly. Our natural reaction is to respond with anger and punishment, but this will not teach our children how to behave respectfully. As a matter of fact, when our children are disrespectful, we are often disrespectful back: "Don't you talk to me that way, young lady!" There are much more effective ways to teach your children respectful behavior!

As with many aspects of behavioral development, your primary method for influencing your children is modeling. Look around you next time you're out in public. You will be amazed at how many examples of disrespect you see between parents and children. Recently, I was shopping with my children. We were standing in the check-out line behind a man with his eight- or nine-year-old son. The boy was rolling the cart back and forth until he bumped his father in the ankles with the cart. The man shouted, "What's the matter with you? Can't you behave for one minute?" Then the man pushed his son rudely away from the cart, took hold of the handle, looked at me, rolled his eyes and said, "Kids!" I had to bite my tongue to stop myself from saying, "Parents!" I don't have to have ESP to know that this boy will have trouble learning how to be respectful. It is extremely important that we model the respectful behavior we expect of our children.

It can be shocking when your child sasses you, calls you a name, argues with you, or uses a purposefully disrespectful tone of voice. You are right in saying that you cannot control your daughter's mouth. You can, however, control whether you listen to it or not. It takes two to argue! Don't give your daughter the fertile ground for developing an argument. Instead, make a meaningful exit statement: "I will be happy to listen to you when you can show me some respect." And then leave the room. If your child follows you, go into a bathroom and lock the door. Later, at an emotionally neutral time, have a discussion with your child about the incident. Be specific in explaining what you mean by "respect." You may also decide to impose a consequence for further incidents. This is a good behavior to bring under control with "Behavior Baseball" (see Chapter 4).

Q: What's the cure for the "gimmees"? My children never seem satisfied with what they have—they always want more. It's so frustrating! And the gimmees always seem to grow out of proportion when we are in a store, with so many temptations. I want my children to have the things I didn't have, but I don't want to spoil them. How can I get them to appreciate what they have?

A: Learning the difference between *wants* and *needs* is an important step in developing maturity. (Many adults with extremely high credit card limits still haven't learned!) We can help our children learn to control their desires by first *acknowledging* them. When a child says, "I want this doll!" the typical response is, "You don't need another doll. You already have three that you don't even play with!" This kind of response does not help her understand her own desires. (What if you were shopping with your mate and said, "I really like these pants," and the response was, "You don't need another pair of pants. You have a whole closetful of pants that you don't even wear!") A better response to the child who says, "I want this doll!" could be, "She sure is pretty. It would be fun to have anything you wanted in this toy store, wouldn't it?" You might even encourage her imagination with a fantasy: "Wouldn't it be fun if the store gave us a super-big cart and told us we could fill it up with anything we wanted for free? What would you pick?" One idea that works exceptionally well to quiet the "gimmees" is the wish list. When your child says, "I want this doll!", you can take out a pen and paper and say, "Okay, I'll write it on your wish list. Do you want the one with brown hair, or the one with black hair? The blue dress or the green dress? Okay. Good. I have it written down. Maybe for your birthday you might get her." Often, just the act of seeing you write it down validates a child's desire, and allows her to move forward. In addition to handling your child's requests in this way, remember to prepare in advance for a shopping trip. Let your child know, before you go in the store, what you will or will not buy that day. Having a clear expectation up front will help your children control their requests.

Children need training in the value of money, and the ways in which we decide how to spend it. When your children want you to buy something, resist the temptation to say, "We can't afford it." That only teaches a child that if you could, you would buy it! Instead say, "We choose not to spend our money on that." And then discuss the things you *do* choose to spend your money on. Children who receive an allowance, have an opportunity to earn extra money through special chores, and have the privilege of spending their money on something they want will develop a greater understanding of the value of money, and the value of good choices.

Q: I am sick and tired of cleaning up after my kids! Toys, baseball mitts, homework, craft supplies, Play-doh, dirty socks . . . it never ends! All I seem to do is pick up after everyone else. I'm at the end of my rope, and ready to give away all the toys.

A: Don't give up yet! There are actually many ideas that can help you through this very common dilemma. Typically, *we* create this problem without even being aware of it! How? By giving our kids too much stuff. Kids today have far too many toys and too much junk. It seems that the more stuff they have, the less they play with it! It becomes nothing more than clutter and junk that fills up the toy-box and closet. When the choices and clutter become overwhelming, a child just sifts through the junk to locate his favorite things. Everything else is treated with disrespect.

My first suggestion is that you spend a day, when your child is not at home, to sort through all the "stuff." Pick out all the favorite items that actually get played with on a regular basis—and box up everything else for storage (or, if you're really daring, have a garage sale, or give it away to needy families). Then take the favorites and create an organized place for them. I suggest boxes, tubs, or laundry baskets all lined up for easy cleanup. You can label the boxes if you like: blocks, books, animals, Legos, and so on.

The next step is to create a daily routine for cleanup. Ideally, you should pick a time that your children can observe every day. Children do better when the mess doesn't get out of control: a day's worth of mess is manageable, a week's worth of mess is overwhelming. Once you agree on cleanup time—for example, every day after the dinner dishes are done—it will take about 30 days for the habit to stick. After that, a simple reminder should keep the kids on track. Children from about age three are very capable of following a cleanup routine. You can help and motivate at first; but if you gradually move yourself out of the picture, you will find the kids cleaning up after themselves! This method works just as well for helping children keep their bedrooms clean and tidy.

What do you do if your children won't stick with the cleanup routine? First, you can remind them via choices: "What do you want to clean up first, your Legos or your books?" You can use Grandma's Rule: "As soon as this room is clean, you are welcome to play outside." You can make a game out of it: "I'm going to go upstairs. I wonder if any little brownies will appear and clean up before I come back down?" (Then make a big deal over the "surprise" when you return.) There are lots of creative solutions you can try. Here's what Rick and Tracie did:

> We have four children, Brian, age 12, Daniel, age 9, Timothy, age 7, and Jennifer, age 4. We were tired of having all the kids' toys and stuff all over the house. One night, Rick told the children that anything left lying around after they went to bed would be put in a laundry basket in the garage. In order to "release" an item from the basket, they would have to pay a 25-cent fine, or do a household chore. It's amazing how cooperative the kids become when they see their shoes, baseball mitt, or favorite toy in the basket! Even Jennifer will come up to me and say, "Mommy, I want to play with my doll, and she's in the basket. What chore can I do?" It's been a great opportunity to teach her how to set the table or put the silverware in the dishwasher!

A variation on the "penalty box" is to have the abandoned items put away until "next Saturday."

Q: My children's eating habits are atrocious! They snack the minute they get in the door after school, they snack from then until dinnertime, and then they say they aren't hungry when we sit down to eat. They pick at whatever I serve, and then two hours later they complain that they're hungry! In addition, they turn up their noses at anything I put on the table, and are always asking me to make something else! How can I get control of the mealtimes in our house?

A: I find that most families have troubles relating to food because parents try to feed their children according to the adult meal schedule: three square meals. Children burn up a lot of energy in activity and growing. They really need to refuel every two to three hours. Most kids walk in the door after school and aim directly for the kitchen. There are a number of ways to modify your routine to make it fit everyone's needs and wants:

Create a snack-cabinet full of healthy choices. Post a note on the front of the door stating the times when snacks may be eaten.

Change dinnertime to an earlier hour. If you don't care to eat early, you can feed the children separately, and they can join you at the table later for conversation and dessert.

Serve dinner in two segments. Have an appetizer, such as bread and olives; salad; a plateful of celery, carrots, and other raw vegetables with yogurt or a dip; or some other portion of your meal on the table for the kids while you're making dinner. This keeps them from running into the kitchen every five minutes complaining, "I'm hungry!"

Keep in mind that many kids will avoid any food that looks too exotic or too complex. At various stages, kids will tend to like simple, familiar food. Offer your kids whatever you're eating. If they turn up their noses, let them eat something nutritious that doesn't require you cooking a separate meal (breakfast cereal, toast and cheese, fruit and yogurt, and so on).

Relax your attitude about food. The more focus and attention you place on eating habits, the more of a battleground mealtimes will become. Allow your children to follow their natural hunger cues. Encourage them to eat when they are hungry, and stop when they are full. Forcing a child to clean her plate, or to eat just because it's 5:00, can create poor eating habits for life.

> **Q:** **Whenever my kids go to their grandparents' house, it takes me a week to retrain them. My Mom and Dad don't follow a single rule with the kids. They let them eat junk, they don't make them clean up after themselves, and the kids stay up way past their normal bedtime. How can I communicate to my parents about following the rules with the kids?**

A: Don't! Children should be allowed to have a very special relationship with their grandparents. And grandparents should be allowed to enjoy their grand-kids without all the rules and restrictions that applied when they were raising you! The times when your children are with their grandparents should be seen as a kind of vacation for them from the normal rules and routines. By allowing the relaxed relationship between them, you can actually strengthen your own relationship with your children.

This doesn't mean you should let your kids take a week to settle back into their routine. Acknowledge their feelings by saying something like, "It's very special when you go to Grandma and Grandpa's house. You get to do all kinds of things that we don't do at home. But, welcome back! You're home now, and you have to follow our family rules, just like always." Be firm! They will learn quickly enough how this process works.

If your children's grandparents are involved caregivers for your child, it's a different story entirely. If this is the case, they should be acting more in the capacity of "parents," and should be informed of the rules and routines that you consider important. I would suggest the following steps to commu-nicate your feelings:

Resist the urge to lecture or preach. To do so will tend to cause a complete shutdown in communication. Any message you are trying to get across will not get through the fog of emotion stirred up by your lecture.

Teach by example. Modeling is often the most effective way to change someone's behavior.

Be empathic, be a good listener, and ask helpful questions. You may be sur-prised to discover that your parent is frustrated, and would love some sug-gestions. By using good listening skills, you open the door for positive communication. Let your parent express her feelings and needs, while you show your interest by maintaining eye contact and interjecting listening words and comments—"Oh, really. I see. Umm Hmm." Only after she has expressed her thoughts, and felt your positive support, will she be ready to hear your ideas.

When sharing your ideas, resist the urge to blame, accuse, or condemn. Don't say "You always feed the kids too much junk. Why can't you make them healthy snacks?" Use "I"-statements instead: "I feel it's important that we limit the kids' sugary snacks. I'd appreciate if you'd help me make sure they eat more healthy foods."

Offer to share good parenting books with them. It can help if you read the book first, and underline or highlight the parts that are important to you. Approach your parents in a nonthreatening way by saying something like, "I just read this really wonderful book on parenting. It taught me some really good skills, and I thought you might enjoy looking at it, too. I've highlighted the parts I found most interesting. Let me know what you think."

Make peace with your parenting differences. Understand that you and your parents are different people, and will handle situations with the children differently. Differences are not always bad! They help kids learn to cope with a world full of differences, and to understand that there are many different ways to do the same thing.

Q: I know one surefire way to get my kids' undivided attention: all I have to do is pick up the telephone! Why is it that whenever I try to make a phone call, all of a sudden they pop out of the woodwork and demand my immediate attention? How can I get this to stop?

A: Young children can't conceptualize the person at the other end of your phone line. All they see is a parent who is sitting there talking to herself, and looking very accessible indeed. There are several ways to combat the problem of telephone *interruptus.*

Plan ahead. Give your children lessons in telephone courtesy. Enlist the help of a friend or family member, and use real phone calls to practice. Coach your child on how to answer the telephone, how to conduct a phone conversation, and how to say goodbye properly. Teach how to make a call, from dialing to saying hello and asking for the party with whom they wish to speak. Demonstrate how difficult it is to converse on the phone when you are being interrupted, and then show them how to interrupt properly if something really important comes up. Discuss what "really important" means, and make a list of all the important interruptions you can think of. You will need to do this a number of times before your young children will "get" how the phone works; but, once they do, they will show much more empathy, and more consideration, when you are on the phone.

Use praise and encouragement. After every uninterrupted phone call, take a minute to express your appreciation to your children. Praise encourages children to do more of the thing they were praised for.

Have a "phone toy-box" near each of the extensions you use. Keep a special box of toys or activities near the phone for use only when you are on the phone. When the call is over, put the toys away. You will need to be firm the first few times to set this rule; but, once it's understood, the kids will actually look forward to your telephone conversations!

Q: My daughter, Emi, is in the fifth grade. Our problem is homework. She's always dragging her feet, and I have to remind her over and over to get it done. Then she spends so much time sharpening her pencil, piling her papers, doodling, and asking me questions that it takes up half the evening! How can we get control of this problem?

A: Let's start by correcting your perception of the problem. You say it is "our" problem. Not. It is Emi's problem! It's time that you hand over the responsibility for homework to your daughter. Experts give the following advice for the most effective approach to homework success:

Give the Child Responsibility and Ownership of Her Homework

This is one time in parenting when you can be proud of the things you *don't* do. Don't hover! Don't overmanage! Don't get too involved! Let your child take full responsibility, even if this means learning a few lessons "the hard way."

Child:	I forgot my spelling book, and we have a big test tomorrow.
Parent:	(Sadly) Oh, dear.
Child:	But I'll flunk the test!
Parent:	That won't be any fun.
Child:	You *have* to drive me to school to get my book!
Parent:	(Sadly) Sorry, I have other plans tonight. Maybe you can think of another solution. Good luck!

Chances are greater that this child will remember her spelling book next week after this episode than if the parent had driven to school lecturing her all the way there about responsibility. Keep in mind that if you have a responsible child who usually remembers her work, it is perfectly okay to help out once in a while. But for the child who consistently "forgets," and waits for someone to rescue her, there is no better way to teach a valuable lesson than to let natural consequences do the job for you.

Let Your Child Choose How, When, and Where to Do Homework—Be a Counselor and a Coach

Sit down with your child and help her decide on a homework routine. After school? After dinner? At the kitchen table or her desk? When a routine is established, let the child adhere to it with a brief reminder from you. ("Emi, the dinner table is cleared—homework time.") Then be quiet. Please—no nagging. Nagging makes homework your problem, silence keeps it your daughter's. If Emi then "forgets," she will have to deal with the natural consequences, which will result in a powerful lesson.

I suggest that you call the teacher in advance, and let her know what you are up to. Tell her that Emi is now taking over control of her homework, and you will support the teacher being firm in the consequences for not handling it properly. If your child continues to have a problem, let her know that you will be available to help her with her schedule—all she needs to do is ask.

Limit Your Involvement in Your Child's Homework, But Stay Interested

Interest and involvement are two distinctly different things. Interest means being aware of what your child is studying, looking over finished work to provide praise and encouragement, and being nearby to help when needed. Your involvement, however, should be limited to helping your child understand the instructions, demonstrating how to do a problem, checking over her completed work, or quizzing her on facts in advance of a test.

Help only when help is asked for—and then it should be brief and encouraging. If your child is requiring more extensive help from you, one of two things may be the problem. One, your child has made a habit of relying on your help, and will need to be weaned; or, two, there is a problem at school that requires a conference with her teacher or counselor.

Avoid Homework-Related Rewards and Punishments

Using rewards or punishments takes the focus away from the learning process. A child can become so involved in trying to earn a reward, or avoid a punishment, that it *creates* problems. Homework is a necessary part of school, and should be treated as such, with minimum emotion.

Focus on What Your Child Has Done Right

It can be frustrating and defeating for someone always to be pointing out what you have done wrong, or how you could have done better. One of the traits of successful people is the ability to see and appreciate their good qualities, and learn from their mistakes. When you review your child's work, it's important to focus on what has been done right. Find something to compliment—even if it's the neat, even spacing of her printing! Children will tend to respond positively to praise and encouragement, because it helps them see their good points. By understanding their strengths, they can find enough motivation to build on them, and the self-confidence to acknowledge and shore up their weaknesses.

Communicate to Your Child That She Is Important to You and Loved, No Matter What Her Grades Are in School

Communicate that her effort and attitude are more important than her grades.

When my daughter brings home her report card, we fold down the top part of the report, and look only at the part that grades attitude, effort, cooperation, and timeliness. We review each item one at a time. I make a comment on the importance of each one, and give her praise and make positive comments. Because each area brings her high marks, I then tell her, "Angela, this is the most important part of your report card. This tells me you are working hard, concentrating, and following directions, and that you have a positive attitude. Whatever the rest of this report card looks like is okay, because I now know you are doing your best."

When you review the rest of the report card, discuss each mark individually. If it needs improvement, problem-solve with your child on how this can be done. If the grade is good, make positive comments, but don't go overboard! You don't want your child to think that your love for her, or her personal value, is conditional upon her getting high grades.

Above all, make sure your child knows that you are there to support, encourage, and guide her, but that you believe she has it in her to handle her own schoolwork with success.

Q: In the middle of a tantrum, Jason, my four-year-old actually yelled the "F" word. I was so shocked! Where did this behavior come from? What am I doing wrong? How do I stop this?

A: Calm down, sit down, and let's talk a minute. Young children learn much about life from modeling. Typically, if a child has heard swear words, they have been uttered by an adult during an emotional outburst. Perhaps your son heard this word from an adult who hit his finger with a hammer, lost an entire document on the computer, or made a wrong turn onto the freeway. However he heard it, your son doesn't know what F—— means, he just knows it's a loud word to use in a time of anger or frustration. Being a young "myna bird," he's simply echoing the adults or older children he has heard. Understanding this, let's look at an appropriate response to Jason's outburst:

> Parent: Jason. That is not a word children use. You can say *"sufferin' succotash"* instead. (Uses the same volume and tone that were used for the swear word)

Note that the parent can direct the outcome of the situation through a calm and thoughtful response. When you overreact, you actually *encourage* a child to continue using bad language, because he thinks, "Wow! That sure is a powerful word." By calmly giving him a reason why he cannot use the swear word—and, more importantly, by suggesting an alternative—you can curb your child's desire to use such language.

If a child is older and actually *does* understand the meaning, or the intended meaning, of a swear word, you can handle the situation differently. First, understand that using bad language is a sort of rite of passage that kids go through on their way to adulthood. I can remember this scene from my fifth-grade memory bank:

> I was walking home from school with three of my friends. They were teasing me, and calling me "Goodie Two Shoes," because I was always so polite and never swore. They were daring me to say a bad word, and laughing at me because I wouldn't. I remember the sick feeling in the pit of my stomach, and the desire to have these kids like me. So, a few moments later, when the strap on my book-pack broke, I quietly said, "Shit." My three friends clapped, shouted, danced around, and playfully punched me in the arm. I was accepted! It felt so good that I found three more reasons to say "Shit" on the way home—each one gaining the same reaction from my friends.

We don't want our children to use bad language, but most kids will experiment with it. It's best to respond in a calm manner: "That language is unacceptable. I'll be happy to listen to you when you can use more polite language." This might be a good time to have a sit-down chat about language with your child. Explain your viewpoint about the topic in a nonthreatening way. Remember to gear *your* language to your child's age. Your talk might go something like this if you were speaking to a 12-year-old:

Mark, some people use swear words when they talk. Some of these people don't feel very good about themselves—they have low self-esteem. Some of them are just trying to sound important or powerful. And many of them have had such a poor education, and have read so little, that they don't have a lot of words at their disposal to describe their feelings and experiences. The problem with bad language is that it can cause people to think less of you. Also, you should know right now that bad language is unacceptable in our family. What are your thoughts about people who use this kind of language?

Having an open discussion about the topic will bring you closer to your child, and allow him to explore his own feelings, and get answers to his questions. One mother reported to me that she recited to her child in an even-toned voice a verbal list of those words she found unacceptable. Hearing his mother calmly reciting the words he had thought to be so mysterious took the "punch" out of them for him.

> **Q: I have two sons. Mike is seven, and Ian is three. I know that it's wise for me to try not to interfere in their squabbles, but if I don't, Ian always gets the short end of the stick. What can I do to make things fairer between them?**

A: This makes me think of a story from when Angela was six and Vanessa was four. The girls were trying to decide what movie to watch. I was reading on the sofa, when I peeked over the edge of my book to watch this exchange:

Angela:	I want to watch *Aladdin*.
Vanessa:	But I want to watch *The Little Mermaid*.
Angela:	We can watch *Aladdin* today and yours tomorrow.
Vanessa:	No!
Angela:	Okay, then. If we watch *Aladdin*, I'll bring you a snack.
Vanessa:	If we watch *Mermaid*, I'll bring you *two* snacks.
Angela:	If you don't let me watch *Aladdin*, I won't buy you a birthday present!

(This conversation is taking place in July; Vanessa's birthday is in October.)

Vanessa: (With a big sigh of exasperation) Okay. But I'm only
               bringing you *one* snack!

I had to bury my face in the pillow! But, regardless of the element of comedy
in their exchange, both girls were satisfied with the outcome, and four-year-
old Vanessa happily went to the kitchen to get their snack! Even though the
outcome was not "fair" by adult standards, the girls had learned a little bit
more about negotiation and compromise. They also could add one more positive experience to their sibling relationship.

As a mother, I could have marched into the middle of the situation, and
forced the girls to do it the right way—*my way*. But that would only teach
them that Mom is the only one capable of finding a solution. It's better to let
them learn through experience.

As a balance to this approach, if you find that a younger sibling is always losing the battles, you can pick a private time to teach your younger
child some negotiation skills, and give him some ideas about how to better
defend his position. Role-playing with your younger child is often a great
way to do this.

As time goes on, and Vanessa gets older and wiser, I see less and less
of these unfair results, and more equal compromises. Of course, David is still
learning . . .

**Q: My 11-year-old daughter has been begging for a new
bike. Her old bike *is* getting small for her, but something
inside me doesn't feel right about just going out and
buying her these big-ticket items whenever she wants
them. What's the right answer?**

A: Trust your instincts on this one. Buying our children things that they *want*
(which is different than *need*) teaches them little about the value of money,
the benefits of saving, and the joy of earning something they really want.
There is a very good way to use your daughter's desire to teach her a valuable lesson about finances.

I'd suggest sitting down with your daughter and acknowledging her
desire for a new bicycle. Then offer to pay a portion towards the purchase—
say one-third or one-half—when she saves up the rest. Help her problem-
solve about the situation to come up with a list of ways she can earn the
money. Encourage her in her efforts. You can even create a list of special
chores she can complete for cash. Help her create a budget, and a time line
that shows her how long it will take to save her share of the money. Create
a visual aid to help her gauge how she's doing, and celebrate each milestone

along the way. You can draw a simple thermometer, with spaces for every five- or ten-dollar increment, that she can color in or put a sticker on when she reaches each intermediate goal.

To make this an even better lesson, you can set a mini-goal of a certain amount, and take her to the bank to open a savings account when she reaches this first step. An added incentive is to cut out pictures of bicycles from catalogs or advertisements, and glue them to the poster. When your daughter has reached her goal, take her to the bank to withdraw the money. Ask for it in large bills—kids love the look of twenties, fifties, or hundred-dollar bills! (Come to think of it, so do I!)

Make your shopping trip an event, and follow it with a special meal or trip to the ice-cream shop. This *is* a time to celebrate! Your child will feel the thrill of achieving a savings goal for a much-desired item, and this will encourage her to set another goal for herself. In addition, I'll bet she takes much better care of a bike that she has earned, versus one that simply shows up in the garage one day!

Q: Molly is three. Lately, everything is a battle, from how I cut her toast for breakfast, to getting her pajamas on at bedtime. No matter what I say or do, the result is a temper tantrum. How do I get control of the tantrums, and get us back to normal?

A: Guess what? This *is* normal! At every stage of your child's development, you need to revise your expectations of what is normal. And, I'm sorry to say, temper tantrums are normal, natural, and inevitable for children between the ages of two and five—and for some kids, even longer. When children feel angry, frustrated, or helpless, the result is often a tantrum. Little kids kick, scream, and flop on the ground. Big kids yell and lose control. How do parents usually deal with tantrums? They yell, threaten, give in, spank, or throw a grown-up tantrum. A better choice is to plan in advance how you'll handle a tantrum, and follow through with your plan when you need it. Like many aspects of parenting, the more prepared you are, the better you can handle the situation, and the easier it is to keep your own emotions under control.

The Tantrum-Taming Plan

Step 1: Pick a Tantrum Place

Tantrums need an audience to be effective. If Molly is forced to have her tantrums in private, you will find that they are shorter and milder, and will completely vanish much sooner than when they take place in full view of the family. Decide where you would like all future at-home tantrums to take place. Pick a private, small, safe room, like a bathroom, or laundry room. Some children do okay in their bedroom, but some just proceed to take out their emotions physically and "trash" the room: so make a decision that considers your child's personality.

Step 2: Give Your Child Permission To Have Tantrums— In the Tantrum Place

Explain the new rule to your child at a calm, quiet time. Be clear and specific:

Parent: Molly, a "tantrum" is when you are very angry, and you scream and cry and spit and stamp your feet. I don't like tantrums. So, from now on, when you have a tantrum, I want you to have it in the bathroom with the door closed. No one will bother you while you have your tantrum. You can have as long a tantrum as you like, or you may choose to calm yourself down by reading a book or playing with your toys. You may come out of the bathroom when you are done.

Step 3: Follow Through

When Molly has her next tantrum, lead her, guide her, or carry her to the tantrum place. Then calmly say, "You may come out when you're done." If she comes out before she's calmed down, simply turn her around, return her to the room, saying, "Oh, you're not done yet. You may come out when you're done." Be prepared! You may have to do this often at first, but her tantrums will surely die off quickly because of the lack of attention she gets.

This method works with most children, most of the time. But it's important that you know your child, because some children need your help to stop a major tantrum. One of my children had a few severe tantrums that included screaming accompanied by self-inflicted pain (children will pinch their arms, scratch themselves, pull their hair, or bang their heads on the wall or floor to express severe frustration during a tantrum). For such a child, time out in the tantrum room is not only unhelpful, but dangerous. In this case, it is wise to hold the child in your arms and rock gently while crooning calming words, "It's okay, Mommy's here." Only when your child has calmed down, can you even begin to approach the problem at hand. Children who "lose it" in this way need to be taught some methods of self-control in a loving, nonthreatening way, and encouraged to express themselves in words (if they're of talking age). They also need to learn safe ways to express their anger, such as being allowed the release and self-expression brought about by crying.

When you have ridden out the wave of the tantrum, remember—when it's over, it's over! Don't feel the need to lecture, teach, or moralize afterwards. To do so could just start up a brand-new tantrum. Your goal was to stop the tantrum; and you have succeeded. If you follow this plan consistently, tantrums will become a thing of the past.

Q: We're about to embark on a five-hour airplane trip with our two children, who are three and six. I'm already having nightmares about the journey! Is there any way to guarantee we'll live through this? Is there anything special we can do to make this work? Is there any way to even have *fun*?

A: Yes, yes, and yes! We have traveled quite a bit with our three children, starting with our oldest daughter's first flight when she was 12 days old. I have learned a lot about traveling with children, and have shared that knowledge with many people who have, in turn, shared their ideas with me.

Following is the plan.

Let the Kids Know What to Expect

Starting several weeks before the trip, prepare your children by giving them information. Have several talks that outline every detail you can think of. You can weave this into a bedtime story, make an ongoing list, or role-play the trip. Include the seemingly unimportant details—because those are the ones that can catch kids off-guard and ruin the trip! Some of the biggies are: the car trip to the airport, the fact that you'll be too busy taking care of ticketing and the luggage to sightsee at the airport, the long wait in the airport for the plane, the possibility of delays, the requirement to stay seated with a seat belt fastened, the small, funny bathroom, the tremendous length of the trip (five hours to a three-year-old is an eternity!), and the fact that Grandma's house will not be waiting for them right as they step out the door of the airplane!

Make Child-Friendly Preparations

Most kids hate regular airplane food (can't say that I blame them!). Most airlines offer a special "Kids' Meal," which is often a hot dog or peanut butter and jelly sandwich. Just remember to call in advance to order these meals for your child. (When you do, you may want to order a low-fat or vegetarian meal for yourself!) Or take along a lunch-box meal of food you know your child enjoys. Include things that take a long time to eat, like raisins and tiny crackers. Chewing gum can keep a kid busy for half an hour, while helping ear passages stay open during takeoff and landing. Even if you don't pack a meal, take along snacks and juice-boxes, since your child will probably not be hungry until after all the meal trays are in the trash!

If your child tends to get motion sickness, be sure and be prepared with a complete change of clothes for you and your child in your carry-on bag, a large plastic bag with a twist-tie, and wet and dry towels or a moist washcloth in a zip-lock bag. There's *nothing* worse than arriving at your destination covered in vomit. Check with your child's pediatrician about motion-sickness medications, and the dosage that would be safe for your child. If your child has a cold, don't try to fly—the pain will be excruciating for your kid, and you'll be the least popular people on the plane. If you *must* fly, get your child's doctor to prescribe an antihistamine, or recommend the appropriate dosage of an over-the-counter children's cold medication. The FAA now recommends that you use a child's carseat or booster seat on the plane for children under 40 lbs. This is a safe idea, and also provides a familiar place for your child to nap.

Arrange to fly during your child's "happy" part of the day. Many parents plan to fly during a regular nap-time, only to find that their child refuses to nap, and just gets fussier and fussier. Pair off one child to one adult, if possible, to prevent general mayhem.

Prepare a Sanity-Saving Travel Bag

Bored kids make frightful travelers! Yet, I see many families who fly completely unprepared to keep their kids happy. Please! A coloring book and crayons, and the airline bag of peanuts, will not keep a child happy for a five-hour flight. Pack a carry-on suitcase or backpack full of "fun-baggies." These are plastic baggies, each containing a different toy or activity. Plan one bag for each 30 minutes of travel, plus a few more if you have room. Fill the bags with small toys, Silly Putty, books, Legos, Tinkertoys, View-masters, Etch-a-sketches, stickers, markers and sketch pad, games, and snacks. Browse the party-favor aisle of your favorite toy store for lots of cheap thrills. For older kids, check out all the miniature travel-versions of your children's favorite games. (If you're traveling by car, remember to bring cassette tapes, headsets, and travel-bingo, too.) The rule is: play with one activity at a time, keep each in its own bag. Use the baggies selectively during the flights coming and going, and only take them out in an emergency at your destination.

We always follow these lifesaving suggestions. After our last flight, when the man in front of us stood up to disembark, he took one look at me and my kids, and said in a shocked voice, "I didn't know there were *three* kids sitting behind me! How did you do *that?*"

> **Q: Our 12-year-old son, Gary, spends nearly all of his time watching TV. He rarely reads a book, rides his bike, or goes out to play anymore. He gets good grades, has athletic ability, and has healthy friendships. Other than the battles we get in over his obsession with the TV, he's an overall good kid. Is he just going through a "couch-potato" phase?**

A: TV is one of the most significant technologies of our world, but it also poses a horrendous threat to our children. The average American child spends more time watching TV than in any other activity except sleeping. According to the American Academy of Pediatrics, the average child watches 20 to 30 hours per week of television—that's almost a full-time job! Keep in mind that *all* television programs are educational—but oftentimes they are teaching things we don't want our children to learn. As parents, we need to take a very active role in determining how much and just what our children are watching.

In a case like Gary's, it would start a major family war to simply demand that he turn off the TV. Instead, parents need a specific plan to get control of the situation. I would suggest that you take the following steps:

Determine how much TV viewing you would consider appropriate. Usually it is best to break this down into two categories: school days and nonschool days. Determine what system of program-approval you will use. It's best not to allow totally unsupervised watching. (How many of you would allow a complete stranger to spend hours with your child teaching him morals and values that are in conflict with your own? Obviously, none of you. Yet that is exactly what we do when we allow our children to watch hours of unsupervised television.)

Decide on a starting date for the new plan. If possible, pick a time when you know the kids will be busy with other activities.

Present the plan at a family meeting. Don't lecture! Don't present this as a punishment—*don't* say, "You watch too much TV; we're going to put an end to this." Instead, present facts and information about television, and explain why you want to change your family's current habits. Do this in a loving, respectful way.

Make a plan for what you'll do with non-TV hours. When children have made a habit of watching TV, they actually *forget* how to play. Round up all your sports equipment, games, crafts, and activities. Visit the library or bookstore, and pick up comic books, magazines, and books on purely fun subject matter. Plan an outing or two with the kids.

Act on the plan, but don't talk about it all the time. Keep your comments to yourself. Saying, "Wow! You're actually reading a book for a change!" will *not* be heard as a compliment. Remember to be fair. Follow the rules of the plan yourself. Children learn most from the behavior you model.

Be prepared for negative feedback, symptoms of withdrawal, and complaints for a month or two. Hang in there! After an adjustment period, life will be very different—and you'll be very happy you took this important step for your children.

There are a great number of excellent books about television and children. It may help you build your case—for yourself and your children—to pick up one or two of these and gain more knowledge:

Bennett, Steven J. and Ruth *Kick the TV Habit* (New York, Penguin Books, 1994)

Canter, Lee *Couch Potato Kids* (Santa Monica, CA, Canter and Associates, 1994)

Winn, Marie *Unplugging the Plug-in Drug* (New York, Penguin Books, 1987)

DeGaetano, Gloria *Television and the Lives of Our Children* (Redmond, WA, Train of Thought Publishing, 1993)

Healy, Jane *Endangered Minds: Why Our Children Don't Think* (New York, Simon and Schuster, 1990)

Lappe, Frances Moore *What to Do After You Turn Off the TV* (New York, Ballantine Books, 1985)

Q: I feel silly asking this question, but it causes a lot of negative energy in our home every day: how do I get the kids to brush their teeth without a battle?

A: There must be a lot of silly people out there, because this is a very common question! I think when we have to deal with something not-too-fun every single day, it opens up an opportunity for battles—and teeth brushing is one of those things (especially when we have to do it at night when everybody's cranky, anyway!). Often, I hear parents lecturing their children about caring for their teeth so they don't lose them when they get old. That's like someone telling you to save money for your next trip to the moon! Another oft-used tactic, threatening to take something away—like the bedtime story—only creates negative feelings about you instead of positive feelings about tooth care.

There *are* ways to encourage children to take responsibility for brushing their teeth. Try these ideas:

- Buy every unusual type of kids' toothpaste you can find. Purchase an assortment of interesting toothbrushes. If you look, you can find musical ones, ones that change colors as you brush, and ones with your children's favorite movie or cartoon characters on them. Buy different flavors of floss. Create a "tooth-brushing drawer" with all your exciting new finds. Encourage your child to make a different choice every night. Suggest mixing toothpaste flavors for fun.

- Buy an egg timer and have your children brush until the sand runs out.

- Have an occasional tooth-detective day. Tell the kids you are going to conduct an experiment. Put together a trayful of different types of food: bread, chocolate, licorice, corn, etc. Get a magnifying mirror. Gather everyone into the bathroom. Have everyone chew a piece of food, then examine their teeth. Make a big fuss: *Yuk!* Explain that if that food were to stay in their teeth, it would cause decay. Get some brochures in advance from your dentist that show photos of tooth decay and gum disease. Be descriptive and vivid. (These same kids see some pretty awful stuff on TV—saying, "You'll get a cavity" isn't very frightening!) Then have everyone brush their teeth. Examine the clean teeth in the mirror. Eat another piece of food, and repeat the process. (After I went through this process with my daughter, Vanessa, she became obsessive about getting every little particle of food out of her teeth!)

- Children from about age ten or eleven start to become very concerned about their appearance, and how they look to their peers. You can capitalize on these feelings to promote good hygiene by focusing on the social aspects of good health. Talk about bad breath, discoloration of teeth, and the like. Don't do this in any way that belittles or embarrasses your child. Just state the facts your kids need to know to keep them motivated to look their best.

- A few creative parents I know use this technique with their older children: "Regular brushing and flossing will prevent cavities. We expect you to take good care of your teeth. In the future, we'll pay for all necessary dental work, but *you* have to pay for fillings." (Of course, this approach would be inappropriate in the case of a child who practices good oral hygiene, but gets cavities anyway. No child should be punished for his or her genetic inheritance.)

- Take advantage of your dentist as an authority figure. Most children will adhere more to the instructions of the dentist than those given by Mom or Dad. Prior to your child's appointment, talk to your dentist about the problems you are having getting your children to brush. Encourage the dentist to be graphic and specific when giving your kids instructions and information. Also, if your child improves, or is already doing a good job, make sure you put a bug in your dentist's ear to motivate, encourage, and compliment the maintenance of your child's beautiful smile!

Q: I've been taking a parenting class, and reading books on parenting, but I still make so many mistakes. I don't get it! I thought that once I took the class, I'd be a better parent.

A: You are experiencing a very typical and easy-to-understand illusion. The more you know, the more you see, and the more self-critical you become. I'm willing to bet that you are, indeed, a better parent now; but you have so many more gauges to measure yourself by that it *seems* as if you are doing worse. Now when you make a mistake, it sticks out like a sore thumb. You kick yourself and say, "Why did I do that? I should have done...." Prior to your gaining all your new knowledge, the mistake would have slipped by unnoticed. The good news is that just being more *aware* of your mistakes is the first big step to improving your parenting style. You have so much new knowledge rolling around in the back of your head, it can be hard to put everything into practice immediately. The first important step is to be able to know what you *should have done*, because then, next time, chances are that you will *do it that way*.

Good parenting doesn't just happen on its own. It takes knowledge, skills, and practice to become a good parent. When you are first learning new ideas, and putting them into practice, they may seem awkward and uncomfortable. This is normal. Stick with it! You will find that the skills, techniques, and methods will become more comfortable with time and practice. Parents report that the best incentive to use new skills is to see the positive results they bring about. When you make a commitment to improve your parenting style, you will be rewarded with beautiful changes in your kids *and* yourself—and the improvements to your family's happiness will be lifelong.

Parenting is the toughest job you'll ever have. But if you are prepared, if you have the tools and skills to parent effectively, it can be the most fulfilling, exciting job you'll ever have. And as you watch your children grow into capable, responsible, well-adjusted people, you will know that all your effort, patience, and persistence were utterly worthwhile.

Dear Reader,

Choosing to be a more effective parent is an important and admirable goal. I hope that I have given you ideas, tools, and skills that will help you achieve a more peaceful, satisfying family life.

I would very much enjoy hearing from you. I'd love to hear your stories, your thoughts, and your hopes.

I wish you love and joy in your parenting.

Elizabeth

To subscribe to my newsletter about effective parenting, please send a check for $10.00 to "Better Beginnings." Include your name and address with zip code. Mail to:

Better Beginnings, Inc.
5720 127th Avenue N.E.
Kirkland, WA 98033

About the Author

Elizabeth Pantley is the president of Better Beginnings, Inc. She teaches parenting classes and gives lectures at schools, churches, community centers, and other family-focused organizations. Her talks are exciting, informational, and motivating.

Elizabeth is a regular radio show guest, and a contributing writer to various parenting magazines. She has a parenting feature that is seen in school newsletters in 28 states. Elizabeth has been featured in *Parenting, American Baby, Good Housekeeping,* and *Redbook* magazines on parenting issues.

Elizabeth lives in Kirkland, Washington with her husband, their three children, and Grandma.

Some Other
New Harbinger Titles

Helping A Child with Nonverbal Learning Disorder, 2nd edition
   Item 5266 $15.95

The Introvert & Extrovert in Love, Item 4863 $14.95

Helping Your Socially Vulnerable Child, Item 4580 $15.95

Life Planning for Adults with Developmental Disabilities, Item 4511 $19.95

But I Didn't Mean That! Item 4887 $14.95

The Family Intervention Guide to Mental Illness, Item 5068 $17.95

It's So Hard to Love You, Item 4962 $14.95

The Turbulent Twenties, Item 4216 $14.95

The Balanced Mom, Item 4534 $14.95

Helping Your Child Overcome Separation Anxiety & School Refusal,
   Item 4313 $14.95

When Your Child Is Cutting, Item 4375 $15.95

Helping Your Child with Selective Mutism, Item 416X $14.95

Sun Protection for Life, Item 4194 $11.95

Helping Your Child with Autism Spectrum Disorder, Item 3848 $17.95

Teach Me to Say It Right, Item 4038 $13.95

Grieving Mindfully, Item 4011 $14.95

The Courage to Trust, Item 3805 $14.95

The Gift of ADHD, Item 3899 $14.95

The Power of Two Workbook, Item 3341 $19.95

Adult Children of Divorce, Item 3368 $14.95

*Fifty Great Tips, Tricks, and Techniques to Connect
with Your Teen,* Item 3597 $10.95

Helping Your Child with OCD, Item 3325 $19.95

Helping Your Depressed Child, Item 3228 $14.95

Call **toll free, 1-800-748-6273,** or log on to our online bookstore at **www.newharbinger.com** to order. Have your Visa or Mastercard number ready. Or send a check for the titles you want to New Harbinger Publications, Inc., 5674 Shattuck Ave., Oakland, CA 94609. Include $4.50 for the first book and 75¢ for each additional book, to cover shipping and handling. (California residents please include appropriate sales tax.) Allow two to five weeks for delivery.

Prices subject to change without notice.